PRIVATISATION

Issues of Principle and Implementation in Ireland

Other titles in the Business and Economics Research Series, under the general editorship of Dermot McAleese:

Competition and Industry

Ireland's Changing Demographic Structure

Small Firm Competitiveness and Performance

Forthcoming:

Overseas Industry in Ireland

PRIVATISATION

Issues of Principle and Implementation in Ireland

Edited by

Frank J. Convery

and

Moore McDowell

Gill and Macmillan

Published in Ireland by
Gill and Macmillan Ltd
Goldenbridge
Dublin 8
with associated companies in
Auckland, Delhi, Gaborone, Hamburg, Harare,
Hong Kong, Johannesburg, Kuala Lumpur, Lagos, London,
Manzini, Melbourne, Mexico City, Nairobi,
New York, Singapore, Tokyo
© Jürgen Backhaus, Sean D. Barrett, John Blackwell, John Bristow,
Frank J. Convery, Peter S. Heller, Philip J. Kelly, Moore McDowell,
Susan Scott, John Williams, 1990
Designed by The Unlimited Design Company, Dublin
Print origination by Keystrokes Ltd, Dublin
Printed by Billing & Sons Ltd, Worcester

British Library Cataloguing in Publication Data

Privatisation: issues of principle and implementation in Ireland
1. Ireland. Public sector. Privatisation
I. Title
354.415072
ISBN 0-7171-1673-5

Contents

List of Contributors

Jürgen Backhaus
Professor of Economics, Rijksuniversiteit Limburg, Maastricht, Netherlands.

Sean D. Barrett
Lecturer, Department of Economics, and Fellow, Trinity College, Dublin, Ireland.

John Blackwell
Economist, Resource and Environmental Policy Centre, University College, Dublin, Ireland.

John Bristow
Associate Professor, Department of Economics, and Fellow, Trinity College, Dublin, Ireland.

Frank J. Convery
Heritage Trust Professor of Environmental Studies, University College, Dublin, Ireland.

Peter S. Heller
Senior Economist, International Monetary Fund, Washington D.C., USA.

Philip J. Kelly
Economic Consultant, Cooney, Corrigan & Kelly, Dublin, Ireland.

Moore McDowell
Lecturer in Economics, Department of Political Economy, University College, Dublin, Ireland.

Susan Scott
Assistant Research Officer, Economic and Social Research Institute, Dublin, Ireland.

John Williams
Economist, Kleinwort Benson, Bankers, London, UK.

PREFACE

Frank J. Convery and Moore McDowell

Given the extent to which privatisation was adopted as a structural policy reform in the Europe of the 1980s, it is surprising how little of the public sector has been privatised in Ireland. Outside the financial sector the only candidate to be actively considered in recent years was the Great Southern Hotels group. What the justification for public ownership of a half dozen luxury hotels is has never been clear. Nevertheless, faced with opposition on ideological grounds from trades unions, the Irish government backed off from even this modest proposed sell-off.

Elsewhere, privatisation may well be an idea whose time has come; if this is so, it's an idea which appears to have run out of steam at Holyhead. Appearances, however, may just be a little deceptive. Over the last several years we have seen a degree of creeping privatisation, a development by default rather than by design. Instances of this are the emergence of a thriving, if doubtfully legal, private road transport sector, the growth in the importance of privately financed medical care, the spread of privately financed secondary education at the pre-university level, and the explosion in private alternatives to the postal service.

It is easy to predict that over the next decade existing publicly owned services are likely to experience private competition as the integration of the markets of the EC make protected public monopoly positions not only illegal but economically untenable. Such a development will simultaneously reduce the *need* to privatise (since publicly owned firms will be forced to behave competitively) and undermine the case for *not* privatising — since the firms concerned will not be engaged in public service production anyway. As a consequence, it seems likely that much of the ideological controversy over privatisation is likely to decline, and the case for changing structures is likely to be considered more calmly on the basis of the economic dividend from such changes.

With this in mind, we think that the present volume will help to provide the basis of an informed debate on privatisation in Ireland over the next few years. It contains edited versions of papers given at the conference held in University College, Dublin in May 1989. Clearly, it cannot hope to cover *all* possible areas for a shift to private ownership. For example, health, education, posts and many other government services *could* in principle be candidates for privatisation, but are not discussed in this book. The papers do, however, raise and consider most, probably all, the relevant issues of policy and implementation for privatisation, whatever the sector concerned.

The papers comprising the following chapters fall naturally into two categories. In the first, the main emphasis is on the overall issues arising from privatisation. The second deals with the problems of implementation of privatisation on a sector by sector basis. This gives the reader an overview of the theoretical and policy problems connected with the reallocation of the property rights in public sector firms and changes in the firms' economic environment, followed by discussions of the practical application of what can be learned from the earlier chapters.

In his introductory chapter, Moore McDowell outlines the main points of a conventional analysis of privatisation as a discrete change in policy towards public ownership. The principal points which emerge from this overview are (*a*) that ownership as a determinant of economic performance may be less important in the short run than market structure; (*b*) that in the longer term, improved incentives under privatisation will yield performance dividends; (*c*) that much of the inadequacy in public sector performance is rooted in monitoring problems, an instance of the principal-agent relationship; (*d*) that nationalisation and privatisation have major income redistribution implications.

The second chapter, Jürgen Backhaus's essay, is distinctly

associated with corporate capitalism. This lesson is extended to the case of 'mutual' entities such as building societies.

John Blackwell in his essay moves outside the usual reference area of privatisation by considering the potential for such a change in relation to a core area of government activity, social welfare. It draws our attention to the room for improved efficiency in utilising tax revenues by separating public financing from public provision, the latter being one of the bases for opposition to privatisation by public sector trades unions.

Connoisseurs of Sean Barrett's incisive analysis of the foibles and consequences of public ownership and monopoly in the transport sector will not be disappointed by the third chapter in part II. In the context of this book, it is interesting to note that his account of the cyclical nature of ownership and control in the transport industry can be seen as a domestic instance of the process outlined by Jürgen Backhaus in part I.

In his paper on the communications sector, John Bristow confines his attention to telecommunications. He draws valuable lessons from the UK experience in privatising British Telecom. In particular, he draws attention to market structure aspects of privatisation and the continuing role of regulation.

The last paper in the volume, by Susan Scott and Frank Convery, reviews the possibilities for privatisation in the energy sector. In connection with the oil industry, it is notable that in the authors' view a privatised INPC might join up with the oil companies in completing the cartelisation of the domestic oil market. Implicit in this is a criticism of the failure of INPC in public ownership to fulfil the role originally assigned to it, namely to provide a counterweight to private monopolies in this sector. They view BGE as a serious candidate for privatisation, but note natural monopoly problems, and also possible restructuring under pressure from Brussels. For electricity, they counsel caution: the UK experiment will show (*a*) whether there are real gains from privatisation; (*b*) what pitfalls need to be avoided. Bord na Móna as a candidate for privatisation is critically dependent on policy for power generation. Even its current shaky financial position would be undermined if the ESB were permitted to optimise its fuel mix. What would be left of Bord na Móna without electricity fuel supply would be of trifling importance in terms of overall energy supply.

This book is the first attempt to present to a mainly Irish readership an overview of the issues underlying the debate on privatisation in the context of concrete possibilities for such a development in Ireland. To a broader readership, the discussion in the first part of the book will, we believe, be of general applicability. The second part will offer an admittedly truncated account of how Irish economists view the feasibility of privatisation in this country. The editors feel confident that it is valuable as a reference work on privatisation in Ireland, as a general guide to the problems of privatisation, and as an instigator of informed debate. They are not, however, under the illusion that the last and definitive word has been offered. They hope that the debate, in spoken word and in print, is only beginning, and that these papers will serve as a catalyst.

PRIVATISATION
AN OVERVIEW OF THE ISSUES

Moore McDowell

University College, Dublin

INTRODUCTION

As an economic prescription, privatisation is based on an assumption that we can achieve increased efficiency of resource use in an economy by changing the institutions of ownership and control of productive assets. To this extent, the interest in the phenomenon of privatisation represents a revolution in the way economists think and the type of economics that is taught when compared to the elegant, un-institutional and to certain extent sterile neoclassical analysis which was virtually unchallenged as the dominant form of microeconomic instruction and research in the economics departments of the universities of the English-speaking world until the mid-1970s. Central to this development is the study of the questions of how and why public ownership of these assets should be associated with their being inefficiently used. In this connection I will be suggesting in this paper that the case for the proposition that public ownership per se is a source of economic inefficiency has been somewhat overstated.

As a policy option, privatisation is quite extraordinarily divisive, given that it is supposed to represent a reform which will enable a country to obtain a higher standard of living from the resources at its disposal. This divided reaction can easily be shown to arise from the fact that, as with almost any real life policy proposal, it is not a Pareto improvement, by which economists mean there are losers as well as gainers from the change. This aspect of privatisation, I believe, can help us to understand some of the features of the methods of privatisation adopted elsewhere.

As an experiment, at least to judge from casual examination of the results obtained in the UK, privatisation has had mixed results. Most observers, for example, would accept that it has been a success in areas such as hospital ancillary services or long-distance road passenger and freight traffic. On the other hand, reactions of consumers and commentators to the performance of British Telecom as a privatised telephone company suggest little by way of discernible gains to the public.

These observations are made in order to set the stage for the main features of an introductory paper in a volume such as this. Those features comprise the outlining of some issues which ought to be considered in an examination of privatisation, and the raising of some questions about commonly held assumptions and widely accepted conclusions. In this respect, this paper will concentrate on three aspects of the debate on privatisation: (*i*) the source of possible gains in economic efficiency; (*ii*) the necessary conditions for privatisation to yield discernible gains; (*iii*) the income and wealth redistribution aspects of privatisation.

PUBLIC OWNERSHIP AND INEFFICIENCY

Considerable research effort over the last fifteen years has been directed to investigating the relative efficiency of private and public sector firms. It may be disappointing to the more fanatical proponents of privatisation, but the evidence in terms of costs and prices is not at all conclusively favourable to the view that public ownership has to be regarded as synonymous with inefficiency. Reviewing the results of empirical work on public sector performance in the USA, Canada and Australia, Millward and Parker (1983, p. 258) note that 'there is no systematic evidence that public sector enterprises are less cost effective than private sector firms'.

In a similar vein, Vickers and Yarrow (1988) question the received wisdom on UK public sector performance. They accept that the sector has performed poorly, especially when compared with overseas firms, public and private, in the relevant sectors. They go on, however, to note (pp. 148, 149) that:

the major problem with these international comparisons...is that it is not clear to what extent the observed productivity variations can be attributed to the effects of different types of ownership. Over the relevant periods, most studies... have shown the UK lagging behind its principal competitors *irrespective of whether the industry concerned was privately or publicly owned* [original authors' emphasis].

In the UK and Ireland, I think it is fair to say, the performance indicators which have brought privatisation on to the agenda are those of financial returns and product quality. The dismal record of the state-owned sector in this country in terms of profitability and of return on capital invested has been widely chronicled and needs no further repetition. Similarly, there has been a history of consumer dissatisfaction with the product quality in the case of such areas as the telephone service, the postal service and (speaking as a parent) education. Technical inefficiency and low total factor productivity, however, are not of necessity associated with poor financial performance or a quality dimension of output that leaves a lot to be desired.

If privatisation is to be a remedy for some deficiency in the operations of those parts of the economy at present publicly owned, that presumes that the structure of property rights in public sector firms has somehow resulted in unsatisfactory performance. Until recently most analysis of the economic efficiency of public sector firms has concentrated on the efficiency implications of the internal structures of the firm (incentive systems, control mechanisms, resource allocation procedures) or of the external economic environment of the firm (the structure of the market in which it operates, financial constraints or other constraints emanating from government). With regard to internal structures, for example, the public sector firm has been extensively investigated, both theoretically and empirically, in terms of the Niskanen (1971) model of the 'bureaucratic firm'. An alternative approach which has been used is to model the public sector firm as a labour-managed enterprise. Both these models attempt to capture and analyse aspects of the public sector firm which distinguish it fundamentally from its private sector counterpart. Neither is a perfect model, and both depend on the tacit assumption that the publicly owned firm is of its nature so different from a for-profit capitalist enterprise as to warrant analysis based effectively on radically different behavioural assumptions. With regard to external constraints, there is a voluminous literature on the impact on firm behaviour of price or rate of return regulation; the conclusions of this literature can be applied to public as well as private firms. In the growing literature on the performance of the Soviet firm under central planning, great attention is paid to the consequences of the absence of any effective bankruptcy threat. From the literature on the 'Illyrian' firm, lessons applicable to the public firm in the mixed economy can be drawn reflecting the consequences of the absence of contestable markets for the firm's output.

This neo-institutional approach to the economics of the public sector firm can, I think, be summarised in a relatively short set of propositions. The first of these, and one to which few will take exception, is that decision makers in publicly owned firms are just as concerned as their private sector equivalents with maximising their own net worth. The second is that institutional arrangements, especially pertaining to performance rewards, will be critical in determining the degree to which the organisation's incentive system will align the behaviour of the decision makers with the maximisation of the net worth of the firm, which with effectively competitive markets means maximising the overall efficiency with which the firm uses economic resources. The third proposition is that defective incentives will result in what economists have called for a generation 'X-inefficiency'. This concept, introduced by Leibenstein (1966), can be taken as meaning a measure of outputs foregone due to 'slack' in the system: inappropriate input proportions, under-utilised resources, unrequited demands.

Reflection on the foregoing should result in the conclusion that, however apposite these propositions may be in a paper dealing with the problems of the public sector, there is nothing in them which is peculiar to the public sector. Consider for example, the literature on the spread of the 'M-form' firm at the expense of the 'U-form' firm in the UK and the USA over the last twenty-five years. In a review article on the subject, Cable (1988) notes that 'the M-form structure circumvents problems...of cumulative control loss and communications overload...[and] may be seen as a miniaturised capital market...The result... is that capital market constraints on managerial behaviour will be more severe'. He goes on to cite the acknowledged master in this area of economics, Oliver Williamson: 'The organisation...of the enterprise along the lines of the M-form favours goal pursuit and least cost behaviour... associated with the neo-classical profit maximisation hypothesis'. (Williamson, 1970, p.134).

The point here is that economists recognise that in the private sector as well as in the public sector incentive defects or organisational problems can and do cause inefficiency. The difference, of course, is that in the private sector institutions may be more flexible, and are expected to change under competitive pressure. In the absence of that pressure, however, the efficiency enhancing adjustment may not be forthcoming. The same might well be said of a public sector firm.

A more general problem with the hypothesis of public sector inefficiency arises when we look at the issue from the point of view of overall control. In the last decade considerable emphasis in the economics of firms and industries has been placed on the 'principal-agent relationship'. Of particular relevance here is the existence of a mechanism to ensure the economically efficient use of the assets of the firm, control of which rests (at least temporarily) with a management which has only an attenuated direct interest in maximising its net worth. If efficient capital and management services markets exist, and legal provisions do not create free rider or other problems, then it seems reasonable to presume that the behaviour of the firm's management will be consistent with the interests of the ultimate owners of the firm's assets. In a competitive environment, this will ensure that the firm's net worth will be maximised, that the firm's output will respond to market demands in composition and quality, and that resources are used efficiently. Under monopolistic conditions, we can presume that the management will not appropriate the rents, and that the latter will be revealed as the firm's ex-post profitability.

Correspondingly, imperfect capital or management

services markets, tax distortions, legal provisions and the like will result in inefficient resource use, non-optimal output and price levels, and composition and quality of outputs which diverge from market determined optima. In a word, inefficiency. Private firms will behave in a manner similar to that for which public sector firms are popularly castigated.

That must raise the question in our minds as to whether there is anything different in kind as opposed to degree between public and private sector firms. Is public sector inefficiency merely evidence of a costly failure of control arising from principal-agent relations where the principal, the government, is either unable or unwilling to align the firm's performance with established norms? Or could it be the case that what is described as public sector inefficiency is simply the result of a highly integrated principal-agent relationship with incomplete prior specification and quantification of the norms set down by the principal?

Answers to these questions are of central importance in analysing the case for privatisation and in evaluating its likely consequences. A positive answer to the first question implies that the main problem with the public sector firm is the absence of effective performance monitoring. The general presumption of markets having a comparative advantage over governments in acquiring, processing and disseminating information, and a more direct and acute interest in the efficient use of resources, leads us to the view that government as an ultimate determinant of the flow of resources to the firm should be replaced by commercial viability. This is the classical argument for the 'commercialisation' of the public sector. Note that it is not per se an argument for privatisation.

The second question raises an entirely different aspect of the problem of public sector inefficiency. Poor financial performance, protection from competition and the supply of resources to public sector firms at below market prices can all be seen as part of a policy whereby government attempts to determine the composition, quality and distribution of a vector of outputs. The firms are asked to produce at a loss, or to engage in price discrimination, or to ensure minimum levels of household consumption as part of a government policy aimed at redistributing real income as between income groups or regions without explicitly raising taxes and having a parliamentary review of expenditure programmes. In a sense, public sector inefficiency is a method whereby the executive can spend without parliamentary control.

From this point of view, 'inefficiency' in the public sector is not a net loss of output, and privatisation must be seen as involving a decision to alter the composition and distribution of the real output of the economy. A decision to privatise, for example, road passenger transport will lower the real incomes of those using buses at below cost. To restore that lost income will require an overt tax-spending transfer. Cash transfers to households will replace subsidised production of commodities or services.

Similarly, the characteristics of the commodity or service at present produced by the subsidised or protected public sector firm can be expected to change following privatisation, with higher cost attributes being replaced by lower cost substitutes. Quality, reliability and service-type characteristics will be incorporated in proportion to market demand rather that the 'public' interest.

These aspects of privatisation focus our attention on a not widely appreciated budgetary aspect of the process: it implies either less redistribution or increased taxation and public spending.

Up to this point, the discussion has really been more about the use of the market as opposed to government to allocate resources. We have seen that in this respect (*a*) the same considerations apply to private as to public sector firms; (*b*) the 'costs' of privatisation are more extensive than are sometimes realised. What has not been addressed is the question as to how privatisation as opposed to commercialisation might yield efficiency gains.

Gains from changing the formal ownership structure can be expected from two possible sources. The first reflects the replacement by profits of whatever arguments are in the objective function of the commercial public sector firm. Overall, profits are more likely to induce a 'positive supply response'. The latter is necessary if markets are to be dynamically efficient as a method of resource allocation, which requires that satisfying behaviour be minimised. The second depends on a presumption, albeit a plausible one, that the internal incentive structure of the privately owned firm is likely to differ from that of a public sector firm. This is based on the idea that efficient organisations require that the decision makers within it stand to benefit in proportion to the degree to which their decisions on average advance the objectives of the organisation. In any organisation it is inevitable that some attenuation of this ideal will occur, giving rise to the organisation level costs but individual level benefits arising from possibilities for opportunistic behaviour, the principal-agent problem again. Nevertheless, assuming administrative rationality, a profit-seeking firm will contain an incentive system designed to encourage profit-enhancing behaviour. This in turn biases decisions towards economising on inputs, increasing net output and orientating the firm towards profitable and expanding markets rather than static or declining ones.

WHEN WILL PRIVATISATION WORK?

The brief answer to that question is that if the full gains in efficiency potentially available through privatisation are to be realised it is necessary to ensure that privatised markets are contestable. Notice here that I do not say 'liberalised' which is generally taken to mean made competitive. Contestability is a weaker condition to impose than competitiveness. It is also in general a sufficient condition. It has the further advantage that it can encompass monopoly structures under privatisation, which may be unavoidable due to considerations of scale.

Unless contestability is made a precondition for privatisation, any gains will be limited in principle to those arising from more efficient resource use. Broadly speaking, this implies quantities and prices unchanged, but costs of production reduced. To this may be added changes in outputs and prices reflecting the ending of cross-subsidisation. Benefits in terms of *consumer welfare* will be only indirect, and may well not be directly discernible by the section of the public most directly affected by the operations of the privatised firm. Indeed, in the event of non-contestable privatisation we are likely to see the gains from the ending of budget-exhausting cross-subsidisation being offset by the use of cross-subsidisation as a mechanism to deter potential entry.

Contestability requires that privatisation be accompanied by moves to ensure that the new private sector entity is not able to abuse a position of market dominance. In this respect, it would be naive to assume that the mere absence of legal, technical or scale barriers to entry is sufficient. Idiosyncratic knowledge and/or customer loyalty can make entry very difficult. Anyone who doubts this should ponder the British experience with the privatisation of British Telecom. It would take considerable optimism to believe that the presence and activities of Mercury Communications are a serious competitive threat to the market dominance of British Telecom. The American experience with the break-up of the Bell System on deregulation at the beginning of the decade does not give grounds for optimism, either. In that instance, regulations were imposed to ensure that the AT & T long-distance market dominance would not prevent new entrants from challenging 'Ma Bell' for profitable sections of the long-distance market. Despite the court-ordered restructuring of the telephone system, and the imposition of regulations designed to ease entry into the industry, the market leader still accounts for about 80 per cent of the business nearly a decade after liberalisation.

In the Irish context, proponents of privatisation would do well to consider the present market dominance of the Irish Sugar Company, a likely candidate for a sell-off. In the event of the company being transferred to the private sector, what regulatory or other safeguards would have to be set up to ensure an outcome compatible with contestability? For the moment, presumably, one can rest easily with the assurance that, since the Sugar Company is still in public ownership, there is no question that its remarkable (and quite unexplained) success in keeping foreign suppliers out of the Irish retail market in no way impinges adversely on the interests of the Irish consumer.

In the case of a natural monopoly, a government has a choice between regulating the privatised entity (so as to ensure a price/quality/output configuration approximating to contestability) or giving the entity a direct incentive to perform optimally. This can be done in principle by a process of licensing: the stereotype of this procedure is the arrangements for allocating broadcasting monopoly rights by competitive tender. Control of the assets, and the rights to the residual income for a period of time can be offered to competing entrepreneurial management syndicates, with the price/output configuration being the effective 'coinage' in which the bids are made. Before this is dismissed as fanciful in the case of major concerns involving large asset bases and highly specialised knowledge, it should be noted that a primitive form of this type of arrangement has already been used in this country in the case of the B & I Line and PMPA. Furthermore, the pool of potential competitors for the contract is not limited to the local population, since in the case, for example, of the ESB, one could reasonably expect that publicly or privately owned utilities in the other EC countries or in the US would have the necessary expertise to enter a credible bid.

How could we judge whether privatisation has worked? If the market in which the privatised firm operates is contestable, it is safe to assume that the internal aspect of efficiency, efficiency in resource use, will ensue, since market survival requires it. The external gains, through response to market demands, will obviously follow from contestability, too. All that is necessary, then, is to establish whether after privatisation, and in the context of whatever restructuring and/or regulations accompany privatisation, the firm and the market show the characteristics of contestability. In this respect we are asking the same question as has been asked about liberalised markets around the world, namely, do they move in the direction of the configuration implied by contestability. The overwhelming evidence from the liberalisation experiment is that in this sense it does work. Study of the US experience — airlines, telecommunications, brokerage, surface transport — (Bailey, 1986) shows a consistent trend towards a contestability configuration, and this despite the apparent failure of the telephone breakup to achieve a more even sharing out of the long distance market. The characteristics concerned are those described by Baumol (1982):

(a) in any market producing differentiated goods, a wide range of goods will be produced, by single and multi product firms, with zero rents associated with the production of each good;

(*b*) there will be no cross-subsidisation;

(*c*) industry costs will tend to a minimum.

DISTRIBUTION IMPLICATIONS FOR THE PRIVATISATION PROCESS

Before concluding, I want to touch on an aspect of the implications of privatisation for distribution of income. In the earlier part of this paper I drew attention to the fact that the consequences of privatisation for the output and prices of the affected firms would redistribute income among the population of consumers and taxpayers. At this point I want to examine the intra-firm redistribution implications and their consequences for the process of privatisation.

It is, I think, obvious that if privatisation eliminates rents within the firm then those who currently enjoy the rents will see their real incomes fall. It is entirely understandable that they should therefore oppose any move to privatise. It would be, strictly speaking, fallacious but equally understandable if we were to regard all criticism from within the target firm or industry as being based on well-grounded fears of a fall in employee real income. Some of the vocal opposition to privatisation, however, is certainly a reflection of such fears.

In other cases, privatisation is expected, at least initially, not so much to eliminate the rents as to 'bring them out of the closet'. In effect it will create a marketable claim to rents which were previously non-tradable. In the nature of things, privatisation might leave the total value of the rents within the firm unaffected by making them tradable as profits; it is extremely unlikely to leave the distribution of rights to the rents within the firm unchanged.

A government seeking to privatise must take these redistribution effects into account. In particular, it will have to ensure that those who might rationally oppose the reform from within the firm are at least acquiescent if not enthusiastic about the change. This is not being advocated out of any desire to see justice but because those on the inside are in possession of knowledge of the firm's technical aspects and of its market, potential and actual, without which it will in practice be difficult for the government to proceed with its privatisation plans.

I believe that this aspect of the privatisation process has

not been given sufficient attention by commentators. Yet it is demonstrably compatible with the tactics adopted by the UK government since 1980. I refer here to the tendency for the UK to sell off publicly owned firms at a discount, to judge by the prices shares reached on trading. Is it not plausible to interpret this as a device to ensure a once-off gain by a transfer from the rest of the economy to those in the firm who are given prior access to shares at a discount against their market value?

I must admit to having a predisposition to believe that politicians are rational and learn from mistakes. In the case of Mrs Thatcher I feel such a prejudice is well warranted. I conclude that the decision to sell off firms to the market at less than market value is not a mistake, since it has been repeated so often. It is at least consistent with the intra-firm distribution hypothesis, and pending refutation by new evidence, I think it is worth some serious consideration when an Irish government starts to think practically about privatisation in this country.

THE POLITICAL ECONOMY OF PRIVATISATION: PROMISES AND PITFALLS — LESSONS FROM EUROPE AND AMERICA

Jürgen Backhaus

Rijksuniversiteit Limburg, Maastricht

INTRODUCTION

Currently we are witnessing a wave of privatisation sweeping across the entire Western world, even including developing countries. No country has perhaps gone so far as Britain, which is by now getting ready to privatise its water supplies. France, having just completed an ambitious programme of nationalisation, surpassed even the UK in terms of the amount of stock it unloaded on newly expanded financial markets. While the bullish stock markets before the 1987 October crash certainly facilitated these sales, at least equally important were the deregulation of financial markets, the introduction of new market participants, the development of new financial instruments, and the closer international interconnections between financial markets in different countries — new developments that have all occurred in recent years. The Federal Republic of Germany, although not quite with the same vigour, has followed suit and thus embarked on its second large-scale privatisation initiative in the post-war era. The US recently privatised the freight-hauling (and profitable) part of the national rail system, retaining only the loss-ridden passenger railway. In addition, a president's commission has reported on privatisation.[1] There is no lack of further examples.

If we look at these cases, we cannot fail to notice that privatisation has a *history*. In recent decades, Britain excelled in ambitious nationalisation programmes with the same determination as the current privatisation moves. France has undergone two large nationalisation waves after the war and one before. The German case is different in so far as that country has traditionally had a large public enterprise sector which has for centuries undergone periodic attempts at sizing it down by means of privatisation. In Germany, public enterprises tend to come back, not through the front door of nationalisation but rather through the back door of successful state enterpreneurship.[2] Both the outright nationalisation of existing firms and the foundation and subsequent growth of new firms are important contributors to public sector growth in Germany. The Federal Republic of Germany in recent years has engaged in the foundation of a large number of new public ventures. The US began to build a federal public enterprise sector during the New Deal era, but most of its public enterprises are operating at the municipal or state level. The recent privatisation of ConRail followed the bankruptcy of several private railroad corporations which were then taken over by the federal government, consolidated and financially stabilised. Again, privatisation was the consequence of an earlier nationalisation, just the other side of the same coin.[3]

As we look at economic interpretations of privatisation, we notice that they stem from normative arguments about an appropriate size of government or an appropriate range of governmental activities,[4] or they are couched in terms of welfare economics.[5] The first approach fails to distinguish between regulatory and entrepreneurial governmental activities.[6] Sometimes, there is even an implicit assumption that entrepreneurial government is either somehow impossible or undesirable. Such an argument, however, is rarely made explicit.[7] The second alternative reminds us of the economics of nationalisation in the fifties and sixties,[8] but starting during the forties. Here the idea was to conquer the *commanding heights of industry* in order to programme the entire economy in accordance with some notion of a social welfare function and under the assumption that such programming activity was politically feasible. In due course, the commanding heights turned out to be sinking ships contributing to budget deficits at historically unprecedented levels. There is an obvious link between the discourse of economists and these governmental programmes. Again, no country provides better case studies for this interrelationship than Britain. But the phenomenon is not new. We can document privatisation during the eighteenth century and concurring discussions among economists along the lines just indicated.[9]

Secondly, it is perhaps worth pointing out that not even today and not even in the most pronounced cases of privatisation do these actions necessarily lead to a reduced role of the state as an entrepreneur. Often, rather, we see the state ceding large industrial organisations to the private sector, but entering into new enterprises in different sectors of the economy at a smaller scale. In due course, some of these enterprises can again be large. Likewise, the same industries that are privatised are subjected to new regulatory requirements substituting for the previous state ownership. Here, the state changes from an entrepreneur to a regulator. The regulatory procedures open different forms of government intervention into the economy, not necessarily less burdensome than direct state entrepreneurship. Finally, the substantial proceeds from privatisation ease budgetary pressure on the government and thereby facilitate the initiation of new political initiatives. In all these variations, privatisation need not be a symptom of 'less government'.

These observations lead to a number of criteria that a convincing theory of privatisation should satisfy.

(1) It would be desirable to explain privatisation with the same model that can also be used to explain nationalisation. Just as we prefer to have one theory explaining both sunrise and sunset within the context of the same frame of reference, it is desirable to explain privatisation and nationalisation with one theory in the context of one common set of references and not each as isolated phenomena. Thus, a unified economic theory of public enterprise ownership could accommodate both nationalisation and privatisation, and would perhaps indicate which circumstances give rise to which policy. This is obviously a tall order. The purpose cannot be accomplished within the scope of this article. But I hope to provide at least a sketch.

(2) Secondly, it would be helpful if we could gain an understanding of characteristics shared by firms subject to

privatisation and nationalisation respectively.

(3) Historically speaking, we can observe waves of nationalisation being followed by waves of privatisation, again being followed by waves of nationalisation and so on. Some[10] have used the term *cycle* to describe this alternation of policies with respect to state ownership of industries. Speaking of cycles is too ambitious, since there are no predetermined periods between the alternate waves. What we do observe are alternations in the directions of policies, and clusters of either privatisation or nationalisation measures. Sometimes, privatisations have occurred once in a generation, but the recent French case offers an example of two opposite waves during less than a decade.

(4) In many instances, privatisation is seen as a reduction of the public sector in an economy. However, privatisation can also be a symptom of increasing government involvement. It seems important to have a theory able to accommodate these two apparently contradictory phenomena.

(5) Finally and similarly, a theory of privatisation and nationalisation should fit Wagner's law and therefore apply to cases of *growing* government involvement in the economy.

This paper offers an exploratory sketch of such a theory. Section two sets out the main elements of a basic model; section three tries to show how this model can be used in order to explain a number of fairly different cases, notably with respect to the interrelationship between policy objectives; section four explains the alternation of waves of nationalisations and privatisations; section five sets privatisation against a theory and practice of public finance and section six gives a summary and an outline of desirable future research.

A BASIC MODEL

For the purpose of this chapter, let me suggest the following supposition. Public enterprises differ from private enterprises in only one crucial respect: their ownership is of limited duration. This is a fairly new phenomenon tied into the Western democratic constitutions. The owner of a public enterprise is the democratically elected government and the duration of ownership coincides with the current term of the sitting cabinet. After this term, the present government will either be re-elected and reinstituted as the owner, or it will be defeated and its adversary will duly assume ownership. Since this characterisation seemingly flies in the face of much of the received wisdom on public enterprise, a word of explanation is perhaps in order. With respect to the definition of public enterprises, we can usefully distinguish two types of theories: those defining public enterprises by their objectives, and those defining public enterprises by their structures. The first three cases define public enterprises by their objectives.

(1) Perhaps the most common is a simplified applied welfare approach, defining public enterprises as instruments to correct for market failure, primarily by means of (second best) pricing rules and investment in terms of some social rate of return.[11] This conception is a special case of the general definition offered above. The implementation of these policies requires a government that sees political benefit in doing so. The history of such attempts at implementing welfare economics with the use of the public enterprise sector shows that successive governments are unlikely to support the same policies.

(2) A second type of theory sees public enterprises being operated in the public interest. The public interest, however, is a notion open to interpretation. Public enterprises are very pliable tools to serve the public interest in whichever way the sitting government deems to be fit.

(3) A special variant of public interest theories assigns the public enterprise sector to the non-profit sector.[12] As in the previous case, the specific purpose a public enterprise is to serve needs still to be determined for each enterprise in question by the politician ultimately responsible. The only option this view tries to preclude is the pursuit of profit by the public enterprise. For many public enterprises, this characterisation can pass as a correct statement of fact, but it is not a characteristic distinguishing public from private enterprises.

The second type of theory emphasises a specific structure of public enterprises as their overriding and defining characteristic.

(4) Theories of self-regulation emphasise that public enterprises determine their own policies and are largely

industry where we cannot document governmental entrepreneurship. Government enterprises can be large or small, labour or capital intensive, multinational or restricted to a small community, aggressive in their business ventures or defensive, innovative or bureaucratically ossified. This variety is also reflected in the various forms governmental enterprise can assume,[13] despite persistent efforts at developing legal forms specifically designed for public enterprises;[14] in fact they appear in a large variety of different forms under both public and private law. Sometimes they figure in the public budgets, but sometimes they don't. Sometimes they are subject to government audit, but sometimes they escape such control. This implies that governmental enterprises can be used for almost any purpose that a democratically elected government might conceivably pursue.

We can distinguish three main objectives of governmental enterprises which are intended to cover this diversity.[15] Recently, the most important objective seems to be public *employment policy*. State enterprises are charged with the role of providing employment where private industry has failed to provide sufficient job opportunities. Secondly, the diversity of uses that state enterprises can be put to may be captured by postulating that *governmental discretion* is a proper purpose of state enterprise. The public interest theories mentioned above are essentially theories about how this governmental discretion is used.[16] Thirdly, *revenues* from state enterprises have traditionally been of primary importance. While these revenues today appear to be minuscule as compared to tax revenues, they are indeed important (as this paper tries to show), hence revenue seeking can also be included as a proper purpose of state enterprise. We can thus write the following policy function:

$$\text{Max } U\ (E, D, P),$$
with E: Employment,
D: Discretion,
P: Profit.

Although in particular the first goal, employment, appears to be a macroeconomic goal aimed at an economic aggregate, in the case of a public enterprise the aggregate goal has to be translated into microeconomic decisions. The third goal, profit earning by public enterprises, can in principle be sizeable. In 1913, 53 per cent of the revenues of the German Empire and the constituent member states came from public enterprises, which averaged 20 per cent profits on sales for the member states, and 12 per cent for the empire (Eheberg, 1922, p.71). While there are certainly other reasons for the waning profitability of public enterprises, one important reason may have to do with democratic institutions and the resulting truncation of property rights. In a predemocratic system with one ruler or family in hereditary succession, and more or less stable preferences of the rulers over time, public enterprises could *efficiently* be used for a variety of public purposes. The profits accruing to the ruler from the public enterprises could be liberally spent without involving parliamentary discussion. The parliament, of course, had the right to decide on the budget in so far as the income side of the budget consisted of taxes. Public enterprises tended to be off budget, sometimes they were even held in the private portfolio of the prince. It therefore comes as no surprise that, precisely during the time of constitutional monarchies, we have seen an astonishing rise and extension of public entrepreneurship in Central Europe.

With a democratic government, the picture changes substantially. In what follows, I assume that there is either a two-party system or that there are two groups of parties that tend to form coalitions. The analysis is considerably more complicated if there is always one party remaining in power with changing coalitions. This is the case in, for example, Italy or the Netherlands. As a matter of principle, the owner of a public enterprise enjoys his ownership only during the time of his tenure in office;[17] thereafter he has to abdicate whatever rights and privileges an owner can enjoy. This is true for democratic government in general. When public enterprises are to be used for purposes of public policy in a democratic system, the simple observation has a special twist. Let us look at the three purposes in turn.

Employment is often considered a goal of economic policy in aggregate economic terms. When public enterprises are used to create employment, this is necessarily taking place at a disaggregate level. Even if a general, e.g. federal, employment programme is launched, the funds will be distributed to various already existing entities and in turn be allocated to different divisions and departments. This will result in a small number of openings to be filled at a large number of different organisational points of decision making. Here specific purposes will guide the employment decision. Specific persons will find employment. Under standard public choice assumptions, notably maximising the re-election probability, the elected politician or his agent will give those applicants preference who have given the ruling party reason in the past to make such an appointment. The larger the difference for a particular applicant between the wage he can receive as an employee of the public enterprise and the highest income otherwise available, the larger the benefit must have been that the ruling party has received or expects to receive from that particular appointee. As it happens, what benefits one party often amounts to a disadvantage for the opposing party. This implies that appointments made by the previous owner often can be less than worthless to the following owner. The appointees cannot be expected to be utterly enthusiastic about implementing the new owners' policies; they are even likely to subvert the effective pursuit of such measures. Secondly, the vacancies the previous owner has filled are lost to the present owner in the sense that he cannot make appointments of his own. If employees of public enterprises enjoy tenure and other civil service privileges, the only recourse for the new owner is either to restrict his own appointments to naturally occurring replacements or to 'pack' the enterprise with his own, as President Roosevelt threatened do with the Supreme Court.

It is likely that employees of public enterprises in this scenario will enjoy tenure privileges. Since the appointment is here pictured as the reward for specific services rendered to the political party that initiated the appointment,[18] we can also expect that the party wants to make the reward as big as possible in order to secure as large a stream of services as possible. Obviously, a tenured appointment represents a higher net present value of the stream of income received from the job than an untenured appointment with the same wage. This implies that *cet. par.* adding tenure adds to the pool of available appointees or the value of services to be compensated for, or both.[19]

Thirdly, the development of this process over time will

lead to a substantial overstaffing of public enterprises with staff quality not necessarily corresponding to the quality profiles generally prevailing in the industry in which the public enterprise is operating.

As compared to a privately owned corporation, the public enterprise will then be observed to underperform in terms of both quality of service and net revenues generated.

We notice, then, that in a democratic system with frequent changes of government and opposing political parties or mutually exclusive coalitions of such parties in succession, employment policies pursued by state enterprises entail two different sets of policy measures, not only in serious conflict with one another, but also in conflict with the other two purposes of public entrepreneurship, in that these employment policies restrict the role for discretionary policy making and non-tax revenue seeking.

Discretionary policy making suffers from very similar drawbacks. To the extent that the political owners succeeding each other try to implement different party platforms, we can expect that the differences between past and present government policies carried out by the respective ministries under parliamentary supervision and those policies carried out by public enterprises under less acute parliamentary scrutiny will be sharper in the latter case. This implies that even more than with traditional ministerial governmental operations the switch from government to opposition can give rise to drastic policy changes in a public enterprise. While administrative organisations (bureaux) typically have a clear mission and follow established procedures, public enterprises can be used for a variety of purposes. Procedures are typically less stringent in a public enterprise than in an administrative organisation. Consequently, investments, strategic market positioning and long-range planning in a public enterprise do not only have to respond to the sometimes sudden changes occurring in the market economy but also have to correspond to the inbuilt frequency of ownership change. Only those long-term goals on which there is a broad political consensus extending over the entire party spectrum can serve as a basis for long-term planning and investment. The remaining goals can only be pursued during the expected duration of the tenure of the current government. The present owner will try, as in the case of employment, to establish his own policy objectives in the firm with as much stability as is feasible in order to bind his successor. This can be done by means of writing policy objectives into statutory provisions or the articles of incorporation or else by entering the public enterprise into long-term contractual relationships. Both features can be frequently observed, more frequently than in the private sector. Even for the political owner, however, they have the disadvantage of making the public enterprise structure more rigid than befits an organisation to be used for a variety of discretionary policies.

In comparison with private enterprises operating in the same industry, the public enterprise will then be perceived as unstable and unreliable in the execution of its long-term policies, overly rigid at times and at other times surprisingly eager to enter into risky long-term contractual relationships. Net revenues, again, will appear to be depressed (as compared to the net assets employed by the enterprise).

In this context it should be noted that the market value of a public enterprise differs depending on whether political restrictions are imposed on its operations or not. The value is obviously higher when efficient (in the business sense of the term) firm policies can be followed.

In the cases outlined above, profits from public enterprises tend to be low, firstly, with respect to the net asset value of the corporations. Secondly, given the size of the commercial public sector, the revenues thus generated are minuscule. Thirdly, in contemporary Western democracies, the public enterprise profit/tax ratio is less than 1/100 in federal budgets. In earlier centuries, ratios of 1/3, 1/2, or even 1/1 could frequently be observed.[20]

In private industry, profit maximisation is achieved through long-term strategic planning. Stock prices reflect the net present value of the stock which includes not only the expected stream of dividend income but also share values. Even with dividend incomes being low because of off-setting investments, share prices can remain high and present owners, in selling their shares today, will already reap the expected benefits from those investments that are currently depressing the level of dividends.

In a public enterprise, the situation again is drastically different. The current temporary owner can reap the benefits from earlier investments, and in maximising the net revenues over the period of his tenure he may choose a low level of investment, resulting in inefficient labour-capital configurations. The benefits from current investments would accrue to the future owner, here throughout assumed to be the political opponent. Since future re-elections cannot be timed and synchronised with future streams of earnings from current investments, public enterprises will be *impoverished*[21] by successive temporary owners. These policies are not the result of negligence or poor management skills; they are the result of rational use of temporary ownership rights. Different uses can only be expected if temporary owners[22] face different incentive structures with respect to public enterprise.

There is one strategy of short-term revenue maximisation that can yield substantially higher returns than the strategies so far discussed and which, in addition, carries some attractive advantages with respect to the other two policy objectives. A temporary owner is able, once and for all, to reap the entire stream of potential enterprise revenues attainable under an efficient regime of ownership structures by selling the enterprise to the private sector and relieving it of the restrictions of public entrepreneurship. Privatisations can then be seen as an emphasis on receiving revenues from public enterprises; in democratic societies with temporary public ownership rights, privatisation can turn out to be the only efficient strategy available for short-term profit maximisation.[23]

In addition, privatisation offers further political advantages. One of the most intriguing aspects of temporary political ownership rights is that with the expiration of the ownership rights these rights are turned over to the political opponent. If government and opposition are diametrically opposed to each other, this entails a *double loss* to the previous owner, a double gain to the new one. However, the previous owners' decisions, in anticipation of the double loss, are likely to have been taken with a view to containing the size of the double gain by either weakening the resource base of the enterprise or binding it in other ways. Privatisation avoids this disadvantage. By privatising an enterprise, its assets are made unaccessible to the political opponent and the revenues can be spent during the current period of tenure. Furthermore, while the privatisation procedure can be used to accommodate a variety of discretionary policies, after privatisation the enterprise is no longer available as an instrument of political discretionary behaviour; hence, it is no longer available to the political opponent in the future. Thirdly, by privatising public enterprises and turning public sector institutions over to private industry, political appointments made in earlier periods and to a large extent by the political opponent will be turned over to the private sector as well, hence losing most of their political significance. To the extent that tenure remains granted, this will undoubtedly be reflected in the sales price obtained for the enterprise. A privatised enterprise, however, can no longer be used to continue the practice of rewarding political service. Consequently, *cet. par.*, less political service will be forthcoming, with the effect of weakening the political opponent.

INTERRELATIONSHIPS BETWEEN POLICY OBJECTIVES

In order to discuss the interrelationship between the three policy objectives, employment, discretionary policy making and profit seeking, the following matrix will be useful. Since the diagonal is irrelevant, there are six different mutual interdependencies which will be discussed in the order indicated in the matrix. The vertical axis denotes the primary policy objective, and the objectives affected are listed on the horizontal axis.

Table 1	Interdependencies		
GOALS	**SECONDARY**		
	E	D	P
Primary E	x	1	2
D	3	x	4
P	5	6	x

So far, we have discussed the different policy objectives separately. In reality, they tend to be intertwined. Pursuit of one policy objective can render others more or less attainable. For example, as discussed in the preceding section, rigorous pursuit of the profit motive will close the doors on other policy options. Sometimes those doors had already been closed earlier and the temporary owner, at a particular point in time, is left with only a limited set of options. The discussion in this section tries to show that successive processes of precluding different options can lead to radical outcomes, such as nationalisation or privatisation, and that this system can be described as being recursive in the sense that nationalisation can follow privatisation, again being followed by nationalisation, etc. The different interrelationships as shown in the matrix above will now be discussed in turn.

(1) As public enterprises are used to create employment, this will also create specific discretionary policy options. When for example, public enterprises are used to foster economic development either at home or abroad, it is not always clear whether the underlying rationale is primarily the creation of jobs for specific age groups or the professed promotion of economic development.[24] Public enterprises can serve a more ambitious role if employment policies are combined with efforts at increasing the skill levels of certain groups in the population, e.g. mechanics or clerical workers. Such activities may be sensible from a public policy point of view even if the approach leads to meagre profits to be extracted from the public corporation, if a tax base broadening or deepening effect can be shown to stem from improvements in the human capital endowment of a population. For example, we observe that public enterprises such as the Post Office take on many more apprentices than are required for their own future employment needs. While the education of apprentices is costly, this may still be a sound business practice since a large pool of suitable candidates is created for the upcoming positions and good appointments can thus be made, leaving a positive externality to the rest of the industry. Obviously, to the extent that this is sound business practice, we will also observe it being followed in private industry. Still, a public enterprise can go

further than a private one, since the temporary politician-owner will emphasise employment at the expense of profits, and thus choose, *cet. par.*, a larger number of additional apprentices. This example can be easily generalised to include other forms of employment policies.

Sometimes we have seen that employment policies give rise to projects that, while breaking even, would scarcely have been undertaken in the private sector. Again, this can be readily explained when both the project at hand and the employment motive are jointly considered. Suitable candidates for such projects are visible (and thus large-scale) undertakings that clearly bear the stamp of a particular party or ideology. Large dams and bridges or other large-scale constructions come to mind.[25]

(2) If public enterprises are to be used for employment policies, it is clear that this may depress the stream of revenues a government can expect to gain from the firm. The relationship between both policy objectives is more complicated, however. A certain minimum level of net revenues is required in order for the enterprise to make a meaningful contribution to state employment policies. Public enterprises are likely to carry out those aspects of employment policies that are at least breaking even. We can therefore expect even well-performing public enterprises to be concentrated where labour-intensive production technologies are required. This reasoning would lead us to expect future growth of public enterprises to occur particularly in service industries. The Post Office is a case in point.

(3) An emphasis on specific discretionary policies will impose restrictions on the kind of employment considerations that can be entertained; for example, large military or space programmes are often concentrated in the public enterprise sector and changes in those programmes can have massive employment consequences. Discontinuation of a NASA programme would lead to mass unemployment among highly skilled engineers that could not likely be absorbed by private industry. There is an interesting implication of this observation with respect to employment policies. The larger such programmes get, and the more specific the job profiles prevalent in the programme, the less likely is a

discontinuation of its activities *for employment reasons*. Rather, such programmes tend to be enlarged and spread into adjacent activities requiring similar technologies. This process will lead large public enterprises to being tied to very specific technologies and ultimately assuming monopoly positions with respect to these technologies. The railways are another case in point in Western Europe and, to a lesser extent, in the US.

(4) As in the case of employment, discretionary policy making by means of public enterprises requires a certain minimum revenue level. While, however, a joint maximisation of profits and the payroll is almost never conceivable, this is not the case with some discretionary policies and profits. Classical policies aiming at industrial innovation can illustrate the point. Consider a holding company entrusted with the task of stimulating technical progress in a particular country. The holding company starts with a given endowment and can issue bonds. The holding company will then try to start up new companies by infusing new technologies and selling these companies once they have achieved an acceptable track record.[26] By selling these companies, the holding company can appropriate the net present value of the entire stream of earnings expected from the new company. The net asset value thus created essentially stems from proving that the venture is viable. The proceeds can be reinvested into new ventures at successively larger levels. Bond issues will create access to capital markets to the extent that the holding company can establish and maintain a good track record of its own. Obviously, in this case, the success and consequently the importance of the state holding depends on its ability to carefully determine and accurately predict the economic viability of risky innovations. Again, in such a set-up, we could observe stark differences from private industry performance. A private corporation would not be likely to sell off a successful company, since the proceeds from such a sale do not add to liquidity; they are in principle available as bank credit. Selling would also create a tax liability. The private corporation would therefore opt for growth and spread out to many different industries. The public corporation, to the contrary, is interested in turning over proven new ventures to the private sector. There are two

reasons for this preference. Politically, industrial innovation is here assumed to be the holding's discretionary policy mission. This mission is successfully fulfilled, for a particular project, when the sale can be completed. The sale is the visible sign of success and, being visible, can be used as a political symbol.[27] Secondly, successive governments as temporary owners of the holding company will wish to emphasise different projects, in turn bearing their different political trademarks. Hence, there is a constant pressure to innovate in new directions which would conflict with attempts to build a large and well-structured industrial empire.

The role of state enterprises as promoters of economic development and innovation is by no means new. Since this section keeps giving rise to questions and queries, let me give two cases, one historic and the other a recent one.

The historic case is taken from nineteenth-century Prussia and involves the Royal Prussian Bank and the Seehandlungsgesellschaft, the Prussian International Trading Corporation started in 1772. Although initially set up as an international profit-seeking trading company of the United Kingdom of Prussia, its importance increased when, after the Napoleonic Wars, the state could not on its own incur additional debt without convening the estates and seeking permission to float new bonds. The Seehandlungsgesellschaft would therefore float bonds on her own, and channel these financial resources to the state. The activities were thoroughly off budget and only partly audited. The flotation of new bonds was not the major activity of the corporation, however. Its revenues stemmed from commercial activities in what today would be called a venture capital market. The corporation would agree to finance a new industrial venture by subscribing to the stock of a particular company, sometimes taking a leading role; and participating in the profits if the venture was successful. If it wasn't, it seems to have been customary to retreat unceremoniously after a couple of years. In this vein, the corporation participated in railways, shipping, spinning, weaving, paper mills, the chemical industry, in cast iron production, grain mills, etc. It is not surprising that there were calls (from private industry) to privatise the corporation; these were only partly successful.

In one case, the corporation also entered the non-profit business where the proceeds of the Royal Pawnshop would go towards the support of unmarried daughters of civil servants and officers (relieving the state of some of these obligations). The purposes of the Prussian Seehandlungsgesellschaft were thus varied. The institute facilitated state borrowing, served as an investment banker in industrial areas that looked technologically promising, took over some social policy tasks and intervened in the economy in various ways. Still, the Prussian state was able to receive substantial revenues (Lexis, 1901, pp. 659-62).

The activities of the Royal Prussian Bank were not quite as farflung as those of the Seehandlungsgesellschaft, but the overriding purpose was equally to facilitate the financing of state expenditure by floating bonds and engaging in profit-making activities. From 1 July 1771 to 1 June 1806, the bank had contributed almost nine million thaler out of its profit to the royal budget. About the performance during the last thirty years of its existence (till 1846) Lexis gives the following telling assessment: 'Considering that the bank started practically without own resources and that during the last thirty years as a pure state institution it had to work on financing a deficit that was held a closely kept secret, one has to grant the results obtained are truly remarkable' (Lexis, 1899, pp. 189-92).

This case shows that the profit motive could be combined with the development motive, and that even some limited social policy goals could be attached.

The second case is more recent and underscores the vicissitudes of political change. Like most Latin American countries, Chile has a history of state involvement in production. A large body of public enterprises used to be organised in a holding under the name of CORFO (Corporación de Fomento de la Producción) which started out as a market-based development agency founding and developing enterprises to make them profitable and viable market participants. Once a company was operating satisfactorily, it would be sold to a private owner, and the proceeds would go into new ventures. This approach is in line with market-based economic policy.

Under the Christian Democratic presidency of Eduardo

Frei, which preceded the Allende government and in several respects started what the Marxist doctor would then complete or exaggerate, the public enterprise sector began to grow and the companies were expected to assume responsibilities beyond what private companies can generally be expected to perform. Such a rule is typical for middle-of-the-road democratic governments. Public enterprises cease to be quasi-private market participants. They become an instrument of social policy, because they cannot compete with private companies. Markets tend to be segmented into a private and a public portion. The *Unidad Popular* (popular unity) government under Salvador Allende used CORFO as an instrument to organise the socialised enterprises that it held from 'interventions' — seizures of companies from owners accused of unlawful conduct. When the military took power in 1973, it had to deal with these enterprises, most of which had become a drain on the state, fuelling inflation. The traditional option, the CORFO approach, involved rebuilding what had been squandered, changing management and managerial objectives, turning the companies around, and privatisation after they became profitable. Another approach would have kept the companies in the public domain, made them profitable, and used the earnings to service the public debt. These are market-based approaches to economic policy, if the companies are not subsidised. The military government privatised the companies, however, and apparently for much less than they were worth on the books — certainly not a market-based economic policy. It was a political transfer that probably interfered with market competition.

Although this is an extreme case of different political objectives pursued by successive governments, it also highlights the extent to which privatisation and nationalisation are intertwined just as well as it underscores the difference between routine privatisation as a standard policy of the CORFO and the politically motivated privatisation undertaken by the military regime.

(5) The classical mission of public enterprise has always been to generate revenues for government that could not be generated by means of taxation. The relative demise of public enterprise began when the instruments of taxation became sharper and tax yields could be increased. Yet a vigorous

pursuit of profits by public enterprises will under normal circumstances lead to a positive aggregate employment effect. This statement describes public entrepreneurship in predemocratic times. The options created by this strategy are not as palatable to a temporary owner as they are to a permanent public owner. A temporary owner is interested in profits now and in making specific appointments, instead of referring to less specific and always disputable aggregate employment effects of public entrepreneurship. Pursuit of profits is more likely when a permanent public owner can be assigned. Again, history provides many examples, as when the proceeds from a particular enterprise, such as a vineyard or a bank, were earmarked by statute or charter for a particular local public purpose such as a hospital or a school. The institution pursuing this purpose then assumes the essential ownership rights sufficient to ensure the long-term profitability of the firm. One could interpret this standard practice in public finance of creating para-fiscal institutions as an early form of privatisation. The practice itself has been widely used since the Middle Ages. The term privatisation is applicable, since both the particular assignment (hospital, school) are transferred from a public body (the City Council) to an independent institution and the revenue source along with it.

(6) Positive net revenues are requirements not only for successful employment policies. The case is more obvious when particular public enterprises, such as banks, are expected to facilitate the implementation of certain discretionary programmes. If banks, for example, are expected to assist medium-sized industries in gaining access to international markets, the expected beneficiaries will only benefit in a meaningful way if the bank is well managed and recognised as a competent business partner in those international markets to which access is being sought. Even if the profit motive does not take on primary importance, it is always necessary for the effective pursuit of those other purposes the public enterprise can be used to aim at.

THE ALTERNATION OF NATIONALISATION AND PRIVATISATION

Our discussion of the interrelationships between the various policy objectives has shown that we can concentrate on the employment goal on the one hand and the discretionary policy goal on the other. Under a democratic regime, the fiscal motive of profit seeking has almost invariably assumed secondary importance. Furthermore, the profit goal is supportive of the other two goals to the extent that a minimum profit tends to be a constraint irrespective of which of the other two policy objectives is chosen. In order to generate the basic framework for explaining changes in ownership structures, i.e. privatisation or nationalisation, I shall now assume that we can operate in the context of a two-party model where the first party (or coalition) tends to subscribe to the employment objective, while the second party (or coalition) emphasises discretionary policies.

Let us start this scenario with Party I taking over a particular public enterprise such as the the rail network and using the company for its employment needs. The network will begin to expand certain operations, notably services, and show signs of being overstaffed. In due course, Party II takes over and tries to use the network for particular policy objectives, for example in order to relieve the airports, or else to combat congestion in metropolitan areas by expanding the commuter rail system. These efforts will turn out to be difficult, and they will be partly frustrated since the rail budget loaded with high personnel costs cannot readily sustain ambitious expenditures on capital.

Let us assume Party I takes over again. It resumes its old employment policies while, at the same time, still subscribing to the discretionary policy objectives inherited from Party II. Continuing the policy of Party II can be used as a political wedge in order to secure the necessary budgetary appropriations required for the increase of rail employment. Some members of Party II will conceivably vote for Party I in order to guarantee continuation of the former discretionary policy objectives. It is obvious that the cost of the discretionary policy will steadily increase and, barring offsetting cost increases of the policy alternative, airports and metropolitan road maintenance, the discretionary policy initially opted for by Party I will become less and less attractive.

Let Party II take over again and examine the situation. A

reassessment of its previous policy will be likely to reveal that the option initially chosen has become politically less attractive than it used to be. In the example chosen, the ministry of transport will reconsider its position and embark on an airport expansion programme or suggest large-scale new construction projects of metropolitan highways. The railways will experience this policy re-evaluation as a drastic *policy change*. It is likely that, in order to compensate for this loss of political significance imposed on the railway it will be given a new task; let us say it will be charged with the task of relieving the internal system of waterways. New investments will be made to expand the freight hauling system. The railway will perhaps also be asked, given the previous experience, to operate a very modern system with as much automation as possible.

Party I takes over again and tries to staff the modernised freight diversion with additional personnel, making its operations more costly than initially anticipated. The railway may even show an operating loss. Party I, still in pursuit of its employment efforts, will find this objective increasingly more difficult to attain. The difficulties stem partly from the production techniques chosen by Party II and partly from the financial position of the company. These frustrations of political efforts are likely to result in a lack of enthusiasm on the part of members of parliament when they are asked to vote on additional rail appropriations. Some people will suggest that the best way to save the railway would be an expansion of the company by means of taking over related transport activities.

Let Party II take over again. The railway shows an operating loss and is therefore unavailable for additional discretionary policies. The old political tasks, due to the employment policies pursued by Party I, have become excessively expensive and can better be performed by agents other than the railway. Nor can Party II pursue employment policies of its own. The operating loss of the railway makes pursuit of other policy objectives more difficult in the sense that the rail budget competes with other budgets, some of which will obviously be given higher priority by Party II. The political interests whose programmes are denied because of the existing rail budget will try to contain rail expenditures. It is likely that these interests can cover a broad political spectrum, for example when, barring the availability of other revenues, cuts have to be made in the entitlement programmes. Under these circumstances, one desirable policy alternative emerges: selling the railways to the private sector and thus relieving the company of its political constraints. The sales price that can be obtained will, of course, reflect the profit to be made from an efficiently operated railway company with an efficient labour-capital mix and long-term strategic planning. This sales price can thus be substantial, a bounty to be divided among the various interest groups, support of whom is needed for the privatisation bill.

This part of the scenario can only serve to illustrate how the successive iteration of temporary ownership can make the continuation of public ownership of an enterprise less and less attractive. The scenario also explains why we witness waves of privatisation of several public enterprises at a time instead of scattered single privatisations. The development that leads to a particular public enterprise becoming a suitable candidate for privatisation takes time, normally several iterations in temporary ownership. Once public enterprises have become unattractive as instruments of public policy, it is politically easier to administer a comprehensive privatisation programme which will, of course, yield larger revenues than the sale of a single firm. Politically, there are *economies of scale* in privatisation programmes. While we observe waves of privatisation and nationalisation, a clear cycle with a determined duration and amplitude cannot be established. The fact that we observe waves or clusters is due to economies of scale. An entire programme requires less political effort per participating unit than scattered individual actions enterprise by enterprise.

This scenario so far does not explain how the public enterprise sector can keep growing. We can, in principle, distinguish between three sources of growth. Again, they reflect the policy objectives typically pursued by means of using public enterprises.

(1) Discretionary policies (here assumed to be mainly pursued by Party II) cannot only be pursued with existing public enterprises. Rather, it is often easier to start a new company in public ownership in order to achieve a particular

purpose. A new public enterprise has no history, and in particular no history written by the political opponent. The largest number of today's public enterprises have been fairly recently launched. Some of them start out fairly small, and only a few will grow to be very big. Yet, quite a few will grow over time and contribute to the size of the public enterprise sector.

(2) It is often with employment considerations in mind that failing companies are taken over by the federal government. This has occurred in almost every conceivable sector and country. The American rail industry is a typical example; the US government even stopped short of taking over an ailing car manufacturing company.[28] Employment considerations were the primary concern.

(3) Employment considerations are likewise often responsible for outright nationalisation programmes. The British nationalisations following World War II were designed to buy and reward union collaboration in the war effort. The nationalised industries were expressly (by statute) expected to serve the interest of their employees. The German nationalisations (to the extent that they actually took place) were similarly inspired. The same applies to the French case. An exception is given by the Italian nationalisations of the 1930s, which were an unintended consequence of the Italian government's attempt to save the bank system.[29] Yet the nationalised industries were still, after some time, captured by union interests. Nationalised industries are almost invariably characterised by strong union involvement in their managements. This is by no means the case for all those public enterprises set up to serve a specific discretionary policy purpose. Nationalisation is a very specific form of adding commercial enterprises to the public sector.

PRIVATISATION IN PUBLIC FINANCE

In 1954, Paul Samuelson started his 'pure theory of public expenditure' with the breathtaking sentence:

> Except for Sax, Wicksell, Lindahl, Musgrave and Bowen, economists have rather neglected the theory of optimal public expenditure, spending most of their energy on the theory of taxation. Therefore, I explicitly assume two categories of goods: ordinary *private consumption goods*

....., which can be parcelled out among different individuals .... and *collective consumption goods* ... (Samuelson, 1954, 387).

These two sentences are remarkable less for what they assert than for what they imply: the first implication is that public finance addresses itself essentially to two questions, taxes and state expenditures, and that the discussion of state expenditures can be concentrated on collective goods. In such a scheme, neither privatisation nor nationalisation can find its place. On the revenue side, public enterprises relate to non-tax revenues both when they yield revenues and when they are privatised and sold. On the expenditure side, if public enterprises are acquired or subsidised, these outlays do not relate to the production of collective goods, nor do public enterprises themselves often concentrate on the production of public goods.

Although privatisation does not figure prominently in the modern public finance text books,[30] the classical works in the discipline address the issue extensively. Even Adam Smith does so, and he had this to say:

> In every great monarchy in Europe the sale of the crown lands would produce a very large sum of money, which, if applied to the payments of the public debt, would deliver from mortgage a much greater revenue than any which those lands have ever afforded to the crown ... when the crown lands had become private property, they would, in the course of a few years, become well improved and well cultivated.

With remarkable clarity, Smith raises three of the important issues related to privatisation: (*i*) the burden of the public debt; (*ii*) the stimulation of public revenues; and (*iii*) the concern for allocative efficiency.

As we move about in Musgrave's three-winged cathedral and leave the allocation wing, we meet the privatisation issue again as we consider distribution. The British government emphasises this point under the rubric 'wider share ownership'[31] and this issue is also the focus of Molitor's entry into the German equivalent to the new *Polgrave*.[32] In principle, any specific group can benefit by the appropriate conduct of a public enterprise.

And finally, the acquisition of business enterprises by the

state has often been a measure of last resort in order to stabilise either the economy as a whole (taking over the banking system) or a particular sector (for instance the rail system in the United States).

Probably the main reason why privatisation policies do not figure prominently in public finance texts today is their complex nature. Privatisation is not a simple policy instrument, it is a whole package of policies, and the process of privatisation (nationalisation) itself can be designed to serve many different policy goals. The subject matter is difficult to encapsulate in modern text books, and it lends itself better to a case study approach.

SUMMARY AND CONCLUSION

In this article I have tried to show how the two phenomena of privatisation and a growing sector of state entrepreneurial activity (including nationalisations) can be explained with the same model of reference. It is one and the same approach to an analysis of public enterprise activity that explains how public enterprises are used as policy instruments, how this use can be subject to drastic changes, and how successive policy changes will lead to public enterprises being less and less suitable for almost any conceivable governmental task. At this point, they become ripe for privatisation.

On the other hand, the need for such institutions remains, and new as well as old enterprises are constantly introduced into the public sector. This should be particularly observable in times of increasing tax resistance, in line with our observation that the heyday of public enterprises came well before the rise of the contemporary democratic tax state of the Western type.

Thirdly, the style of this essay was deliberately kept at a positive and descriptive level in an effort to explain seemingly contradictory phenomena.

Fourthly, the analysis shows that waves of both nationalisation and privatisation should be expected to alternate. Politically, there are economies of scale in arriving at packages containing several such privatisation or nationalisation bills as compared to the political costs and benefits or introducing a bill that covers just one entity.

Finally, I have tried to show how privatisations and

nationalisations fit into the received theory of public finance.

The theoretical approach outlined in this article is admittedly crude and preliminary. It would be desirable to underpin the argument with a series of case studies involving both historical and international cross-country comparisons. In particular, an emphasis would be required on policy switches stemming from changes in government. In the light of these case studies, is it sufficient to remain in a two-party-three-policy framework? Obviously, the basic model could also be formalised. Since that would be the easiest of the above mentioned tasks, I personally suggest the empirical case study approach be followed first.

I would like to thank Shyam Kamath, Günter Knieps, Christian Marfels and Zane Spindler for their comments on an earlier draft of this paper.

government's budget in the period when the sale of assets takes place, but also in subsequent periods.

Although privatisation has not taken place in any serious way in Ireland, it remains an important policy issue. The public enterprise sector employs almost 7 per cent of the work force and is responsible for about a quarter of total capital formation and total output. Many public enterprises have low profitability and are used as an instrument to achieve a variety of social and economic objectives. In contrast, New Zealand, another small industrial country with a large public enterprise sector, has recently embarked on a major programme of corporatisation and privatisation as means to improve the efficiency of its state enterprise sector.

Section two examines the factors influencing the budgetary effects of privatisation. Section three describes the recent experience of New Zealand and notes some lessons that may be drawn for state enterprise policies in Ireland.

While I have benefited from the comments of R. Hemming, C. Schiller and B. Smith, I am solely responsible for the views expressed in this chapter. Any views expressed should not be interpreted as official IMF views.

BUDGETARY IMPLICATIONS OF PRIVATISATION: CONCEPTUAL ISSUES

(1) *Introduction*: Assessing the budgetary impact of privatising a particular public enterprise requires the analyst to make a number of assumptions, some highly conjectural. One begins with a judgment on the objectives of the authorities in carrying out a privatisation programme, for this will critically influence the type of privatisation adopted (sale of equity ownership, contracting out, liquidation of the assets of an enterprise), the method of implementation (e.g. offers for sale, tendering), and the associated policies towards deregulation and financial restructuring which will influence the perceived market value of an enterprise to potential buyers. One must then make an assessment of the likely effects of the privatisation on the operation of the enterprise or the functioning of a particular service delivery programme. This section identifies several factors which determine the budgetary impact of privatising a public enterprise.

Table 1

Assumptions underlying the polar case

1. A profit-making public enterprise.

2. The sales of price of the public enterprise reflects the full market value of assets.

3. There is agreement between the government and private purchasers on the expected profit stream after privatisation.

4. No corporate income taxes.

5. Full remittance of public enterprise profits to the government.

6. No transfers from the government to the enterprise.

7. No change in the financial performance of the enterprise after privatisation.

8. No change in other revenue or expenditure policies.

9. Full information on prices and markets.

10. No transactions costs associated with the sale of assets.

For the purpose of our analysis, 'budgetary impact' encompasses two aspects: (*i*) the net change in the income flow to the government arising from privatisation, for example, the difference in the magnitude and timing of the net income stream to the government from the privatised enterprise, relative to the situation where the enterprise remains under public ownership; and (*ii*) the change in the net wealth position of the government.[1]

In the usual case, the privatisation of an enterprise involves the sale of the government's equity in an enterprise to the private sector in exchange for liquid assets (contracting, leasing arrangements and liquidation of assets are treated under 9 below). As a polar case, assume a world without corporate income taxes, where the public enterprise had fully remitted its profits to the government and received no transfers from the government, and where all parties to the sale expect that the firm's financial performance will essentially remain unchanged after privatisation (see table 1). Also assume that all parties have full information on prices and markets, and for the moment, that there are no transaction costs associated with the sale. In such a case, the sales price received by the government would be equivalent to the discounted stream of expected profit remittances that would have been received, if the enterprise had remained in the public sector.

In this case, the sale of the enterprise only improves the government's liquidity position, but leaves its net wealth unchanged. The government simply substitutes a liquid asset for a physical asset, which are equal in value. In other words, the government obtains a higher level of current income at the expense of future income. Assuming no change in the government's other revenue or expenditure policies, the authorities could invest the sales proceeds in a financial asset that could fully replicate what would have been the income stream to the government if the enterprise had not been sold.[2] This leaves the government's financial position unchanged except for the *composition* of its assets as between equity in the public enterprise and other financial assets. In such a case, the budgetary impact of the privatisation exercise itself would be nil.[3]

A number of important assumptions are embedded in this

simple analysis which bear further examination. Specifically:

(*a*) In pricing the assets of the enterprise, what does the government seek to attain: maximum revenue? a widened share ownership? employee share ownership? What are the economic factors affecting the sales price of the enterprise? How will the sales price differ from the discounted stream of after-tax profits that would have been earned in the absence of privatisation?

(*b*) How will the financial relationship between the public enterprise and the government change as a consequence of privatisation? This requires an analysis of the likely impact of privatisation on the flow of receipts and disbursements to and from the enterprise (e.g. corporate tax payments, dividend payments, operating subsidies and capital transfers, net lending).

(*c*) What changes in government policy towards the enterprise would accompany any change in ownership: changes in the regulatory environment determining the firm's exposure to domestic or international competition? changes in the firm's autonomy in decisions on the composition of output, employment levels or pricing policy?

(*d*) What effects would privatisation have on efficiency and profitability of the enterprise's performance, independent of changes in government policy?

(*e*) How are the sales proceeds used? Do they reduce the government's net borrowing requirement? Are they spent or used to lower tax rates?

(*f*) What are the effects of a privatisation programme on the domestic capital market for equities and bonds? Is foreign investment politically acceptable?

(*g*) Do the results differ for a chronic loss-making firm?

(*h*) What approach does the government follow in transacting the sale?

(2) *Determining the sales price of the public enterprise*: In the period when the transfer of ownership takes place, the fiscal impact of privatisation will principally reflect the proceeds received from the sale of the enterprise. The financial profitability of the firm will obviously influence the perceptions of the market as to its value, although the observed financial status is only a partial and often inaccurate

measure of potential profitability or economic performance.

Define S_1 as the discounted value of the expected stream of after-tax remittances that would have been received if the enterprise had not been privatised. In principle, the government should be unwilling to accept less than an amount equal to S_1, or the liquidation value of the assets of the firm, whichever is higher.[4] Any lower amount would leave the government worse off, for example, its net worth position would decline (regardless of the time period over which this flow in income is received).

The maximum it could seek, S_m, would be the discounted value of the expected stream of after-tax remittances that could be realised as a result of privatisation. An improvement in profit stream may reflect the effects of private management reforms or associated changes in the economic environment of the enterprise due to government policy actions. Alternatively, it may reflect specific actions taken by the government to enhance the market value of the enterprise (perhaps through limits on competition). In assessing the overall fiscal impact, it is important to distinguish between these cases (see 5 and 8 below).

The private purchasers of an enterprise's assets will inevitably form their own views on their value, reflecting expectations of the current financial status of the enterprise, the prospects for improved profitability, their personal discount rate and degree of risk aversion, the likelihood of a favourable change in the policy environment and the potential liquidation value of the firm's land, plant and equipment. The ultimate sales price (depending on the transaction method for the sale) will reflect these differing views and other factors related to the capital market conditions (e.g. its size) under which the government needs to market an enterprise's assets.

There are a number of factors that may dampen the sales price, even to levels below S_1 (in situations where the asset liquidation value is not higher than S_1). Some argue that since private entrepreneurs can spread risk less readily than the government and are more risk averse, they will be unwilling to pay even S_1. Private purchasers generally face a higher cost of capital than sovereign governments, and thus may discount future profits by more than the government, leading to a lower offer price. Bös (1988) notes that information asymmetries across investors and the government may also lead to underpricing of new equity issues.

Finally, political factors or legal requirements may lead the government to set the issue price or offer price at a lower than desirable level for 'fear of losing political support for the privatisation campaign if too many shares remain unsold'[5] or if the share issuance is not sufficiently widespread. It is generally accepted that a significant underpricing of shares occurred in the British privatisation programme.

Based on the above analysis, one would expect that there is a risk that the sale price may be less that S_1, unless one can obtain improvements in profitability sufficient to offset the negative factors discussed above. This would lead to a *reduction* in the government's net worth.

(3) *Transaction costs of privatisation*: Governments have used different methods of selling public assets, including offers for sale and tender offers. These methods have proven difficult to use, even in countries where capital markets are well developed. They may be even more problematical in developing countries where capital markets are thin, thus limiting the possibility of offering public assets on the domestic capital market. Yet fears of foreign economic domination may lead the government to limit foreign equity holdings or the sale of public enterprises on international capital markets.

Many observers of the British privatisation programme have argued that the particular approach taken in selling assets proved quite costly in terms of the receipts from privatisation (see Vickers and Yarrow, pp.171-180, and Buckland). In particular, by relying on 'offers for sale' at prices that were quite conservatively set, the proceeds were considerably less than would have been received if the shares had been offered on tender, and if the sales had been tranched so as to allow an initial market valuation on a small introductory issue of equity. Buckland argues that the resulting underpricing relative to market values 'can be identified as the "price" of meeting the government's other objectives' (Buckland, p.244), and that such underpricing led to foregone receipts ranging from £600 to £1300 million.

Vickers and Yarrow (1989) suggest that the undervaluation on offers of sale (in terms of a comparison of the price at the end of the first trading day relative to the initial tender offer price) exceeded £3.5 billion on sales between 1981 and July 1987.

Buckland argues that the more limited use of tenders reflects the authorities' desire for greater scope in managing the shareholder list to ensure an initially more widespread ownership. Vickers and Yarrow argue (p.178) that

> Underpricing is a way of encouraging wider share ownership, it avoids political embarrassment, and it minimises the chances that individual investors (who have votes) will sustain capital losses. Underpricing is also greatly to the benefit of the City institutions. Some degree of underpricing on average is probably inevitable once the Government has decided to sell such large portions of equity at a time...But there was nothing inevitable about its extent in the major privatisations, nor did the Government have to sell shares in that fashion.

Mayer and Meadowcroft also argue that the underwriting costs have been excessive, and that in many respects the government is in a better position to absorb the risk of underwriting than the private sector, since it does not face the cash flow constraint of a private underwriting firm. In the words of Vickers and Yarrow (p.183), 'underwriting is all the more mysterious in view of the evident generosity with which the major privatised issued were priced'.

(4) *Financial interactions with and without privatisation*: The government and the public enterprise sector interact financially in a number of ways, and these may differ from the assumptions in table 1. On the one hand, the government may finance the operations of public enterprises through subsidies, capital transfers, net lending, and equity injections. On the other hand, public enterprises may contribute to budget revenues through tax, dividend, and debt service payments. The budgetary impact in the period following privatisation represents the change in the net stream of these payments to and from the budget, along with any changes in interest outlays or receipts stemming from the use of the sales proceeds. Account should also be taken of indirect financial

links that do not show up explicitly in the government's budget, but which may be quantitatively significant, for example, government guarantees of public enterprise debts, externality effects on other enterprises, and in the case of many developing countries, payments arrears.

(*a*) *Corporate income taxation*: the polar case assumed no corporated income taxation. If private enterprises are subject to taxation on their operating profits, the government would then receive some of its income from the privatised enterprise in the form of corporate tax payments, rather than as an upfront payment reflected in the sales price. The sales proceeds would presumably reflect the discounted stream of *after-tax* profits following privatisation. Where tax evasion is common, and the government is unable to ascertain the 'true' profit situation, the government may be the net loser from privatisation by virtue of a lower sales price and lower subsequent corporate tax receipts. Where the purchaser is a foreign company, tax evasion may also imply a leakage of profits outside the domestic economy.

(*b*) *Profit remittances*: in principle, full privatisation would lead to a shift in profit remittances from the government budget to the private shareholders. If the after-tax profits of a public enterprise are not fully remitted to the government, the presumption is that such retained earnings are used for reinvestment in the enterprise, thus leading to an increase in its net worth. In the event of privatisation, the sales price for the enterprise would be unaffected, and would still reflect the discounted stream of expected after-tax profits.

Privatisation would still lead to the government receiving its revenues in the present, at the expense of a loss in such property income in the future. The only difference arising from a practice of less than full remittance would be that the loss of such future property incomes over the medium term would be less.

In practice, these assumptions are not always valid. When a public enterprise is a monopoly under regulation, it may have an incentive to over-invest; by expanding its capital base (on which the rate of return is based) it may increase absolute profits. The investment may then not lead to a commensurate increase in net worth. In many countries, governments have difficulty in extracting dividends from corporations, and in the case of industries with a strong cash flow, over-investment often occurs.

One should note that from a budgetary perspective, it is irrelevant whether the government receives the excess of a public enterprise's income over its costs in the form of profit transfers or tax payments. From the enterprise's point of view, however, a profit tax exemption may lead it to believe that its operations are more profitable than is actually the case, possibly slowing its efforts to seek out new opportunities and improve efficiency.

Most governments engage in net lending operations with the public enterprise sector, and in principle this results in subsequent interest receipts to the government's budget. The amount of interest income from public enterprises will be determined by the level of outstanding credit and the interest rate the government charges. Sometimes the government offers more lenient terms in its loans to public enterprises than those at which it borrows, resulting in a subsidy to the borrower.[6] While a cost borne by the government, the subsidy will be unaffected by privatisation.

(*c*) *Current transfers or subsidies to the public enterprise:* to appraise the impact of privatisation on such transfers requires an assessment of why they are made. Leaving aside the situation of the loss-making public enterprise due to inefficiencies, such subsidies typically relate to the pursuit of government policy objectives (e.g. low prices for foodstuffs or utilities, employment targets, regional development priorities) independent of the enterprise's commercial objectives. If privatisation leads to a termination of such transfers, this would probably reflect the government's decision to abandon using the enterprise to realise such policy goals. If the government continues to pursue the objective through other means of equal cost, privatisation would yield no savings in terms of the subsidy.

Similarly, if the privatised enterprise is expected to continue the pursuit of such social or other objectives, the government will still need to cover the associated costs.

(*d*) *Capital transfers and net lending of the government* often finance investment expenditures of the public enterprise sector. At times, the enterprise is investing on behalf of the government, sometimes for noncommercial objectives. Such loans may also reflect the government's using its stronger credit position to borrow externally on behalf of the enterprise; generally, the enterprise will service the debt. The government may also provide funds to enterprises not creditworthy enough to borrow from commercial sources. Equity investments by the government in public enterprises are also common, being used to broaden their capital base. At times, such investments may represent a disguised form of subsidy to cover operating losses.

In principle, one would not expect privatisation to lead to a significant change in capital transfers or net lending. If an investment in a public enterprise is perceived to have an adequate rate of return, the government's motivation to support the investment after privatisation would be no less. The only issue is whether the government chooses to invest on its own, or to provide loans to the now privatised enterprise. Similarly, if the purpose of the loan is to achieve noncommercial objectives, privatisation would not affect such a decision. In practice, however, privatisation might lead to reduced capital transfers and net lending to the privatised enterprises, if only because the political and economic linkages with the government would be lessened.

Another issue that may arise with privatisation is the status of the public enterprise's debts with the government. Such liabilities would inevitably be a factor in arriving at a sales price. As with any other liability of the enterprise which may have arisen from noncommercial decisions, the government probably will have to absorb any loss in a lower sales price. Similarly, in many countries public enterprises have borrowed heavily in domestic and foreign credit markets, with government guarantees. Such guarantees create contingent liabilities which may affect government finances in future periods. Their status would have to be clarified at the time of privatisation. Probably, the government would bear the burden of the guarantee.

(5) *Improvement in the financial performance of the enterprise*: A positive and durable fiscal impact requires improvements in productive and allocative efficiency. As noted in section two, these are important objectives of any privatisation programme, even in regard to current profit-

making firms not receiving any operating subsidies from the government. Several factors underlying weak financial performance by a public enterprise may be distinguished: (*i*) poor internal management, such that under private management the firm's operations could be reorganised to achieve higher productivity; (*ii*) external interference in the firm's operations (e.g. in its pricing, employing or output decisions); (*iii*) lack of comparative advantage, such that the firm would not be profitable under any market test (see 6 below); and (*iv*) market structure, e.g. insulation from the pressure of competition.

By itself, privatisation is only likely to address the issue of internal management. The fiscal impact of improved management may be reflected in the sales price of the firm and in the level of corporate tax receipts. If the government believes the firm will be more profitable after privatisation, it may seek some of these gains in a sales price closer to S_m. If the government realises a higher price, privatisation will have yielded some additional fiscal benefit in the form of greater short-term revenues from the sales proceeds. In addition, the government will benefit from higher subsequent corporate tax receipts from the privatised enterprise.

One of the most important determinants of efficiency is the macroeconomic policy environment within which the enterprise operates. In many countries, fundamental structural reforms in the policy environment are essential for improving the efficiency and profitability of privatised firms. When the government accompanies privatisation with a relaxation of controls on the enterprise's operation (e.g. on the price it can charge for its output, or on the price paid for its inputs), or by exposing it more fully to competition, the benefits arise not from privatisation but from the act of removing these controls or the more competitive environment.

Since the government could, in principle, realise the full value of such improvements in the public enterprise's financial performance without privatisation, it would be misleading to associate these benefits with privatisation. If the government were willing to relax such controls, reduce such interference, enhance exposure to competition, and force greater financial autonomy (e.g. removal of government financing of operating losses), it would obviously make sense for the government to take such actions prior to or as part of the privatisation effort, so as to obtain the rents from such action in the form of a higher sales price.

When the government accompanies privatisation with *restrictions* on trade, in order to promote private demand for the enterprise's assets, one might observe high profitability after privatisation. However, such gains would be at the expense of lower allocative efficiency in the economy as a whole. The fiscal gains from privatising the enterprise are *likely* to be offset by the lower productivity and output in other sectors of the economy.

For an enterprise that is essentially not competitive under free market conditions, privatisation will not remedy the situation. In such circumstances, there is not likely to be a significant fiscal benefit to privatisation. Whatever subsidies have been required to operate the public enterprise in the past will still be necessary after privatisation, though to a lesser extent. The possibility of closure of the enterprise should be considered.

(6) *The loss-making enterprise*: It is essential to determine the source of losses. The government would need to asses the prospects for improved performance in determining the financial conditions for sale. When the sources of inefficiency reflect conscious government policy decisions, privatisation is unlikely to change the situation. In the case of an enterprise sustaining operational losses which are financed by direct government transfers, privatisation would entail that the government continue to provide such operational subsidies.

In such situations where the enterprise cannot be made competitive without substantial subsidies, closure might be considered, with the government selling off the physical assets of the enterprise and settling with the firm's creditors (including its employees). Often the liquidation value of the firm's assets (land, equipment and plant) may be sufficiently high that the purchase of the firm is still an attractive option to private investors. Such enterprises have effectively shut their doors with the assets dismantled and sold and with the employees receiving some severance pay. Typically, the budget is relieved of subsidies in subsequent years. In other cases, the liquidation value of the enterprise may be low, and in some developing countries a lack of budgetary resources to finance the contingent liabilities of the divested firm may be an impediment to privatisation (Nellis & Kikeri).

(7) *The use of the sales proceeds*: In principle, the sales proceeds can be applied either to reduce/increase the size of the government's deficit/surplus (by acquiring financial assets or reducing its debt) or to finance tax cuts or expenditure increases. In the former case, there is a substitution of increased interest income (or reduced interest costs) for the property income stream previously derived from the enterprise. In principle, there is no net change in the fiscal position of the government over the medium term. The sales proceeds would reduce the deficit in the initial period;[7] in subsequent periods, revenues would remain as they were before privatisation.

In initially reducing the government's deficit, privatisation may give rise to the perception of a shift in the government's macroeconomic posture. This may mask the true extent of the fiscal imbalances since the initially reduced deficit does not in fact correspond to any change in the underlying fiscal position, but rather is simply a change in the composition of the government's asset holdings. If the funds are neither spent nor used to cut taxes, the underlying fiscal policy stance would be unchanged, both in the period of sale and subsequent periods.[8]

However, political pressures often lead authorities to use the proceeds of privatisation either to increase expenditure or limit taxation, rather than to reduce the deficit. Such a policy would be at the expense of a higher deficit in subsequent periods, relative to the pre-privatisation position.[9]

(8) *Other fiscal effects*: There may be some indirect budgetary consequences from privatisation. Since it adds to the supply of physical assets available in the private market, the price level of existing physical assets must decline in order for markets to clear. On the other hand, in financial markets there will be an exchange of financial assets, as the government obtains resources form the private sector and, under the assumption above, either reinvests the funds or borrows less. While it is difficult to judge the ultimate impact

on interest rates, any changes will affect both private investment demand and the government's cost of borrowing.[10]

Significant indirect effects may also arise from the way in which privatisation is implemented. Without other policy reforms, the gains in productivity are likely to be limited in size and narrowly confined to the enterprise. When accompanied by liberalisation of trade and reduced controls, the positive effects on the enterprise and the economy are more significant, and this will be reflected in commensurate fiscal gains. Conversely, privatisation associated with tightened controls may yield fiscal gains to the budget and the privatised enterprise, but at the expense of possibly greater losses elsewhere in the economy.

(9) *Alternative approaches to privatisation:* Privatisation does not necessarily imply the transfer of ownership of a firm. In some countries, privatisation through leasing and management contracts has proven both politically acceptable and commercially successful as a means of enhancing the efficiency of an enterprise while retaining public ownership. Under a *management contract*, the contractor is paid by the government for its management services, but does not directly benefit from the enterprise's financial performance. In principle, this should allow the government to benefit directly from any improvement in efficiency derived from the strengthened management. The typical difficulty that emerges with such contracts is that they tend to be on a cost-plus basis, without any penalty or awards associated with a change in the enterprise's performance. This frees the manager from any incentive to obtain increased efficiency.

Under a *lease arrangement*, a private operator leases an asset or facility owned by the government and uses it to conduct business on its own account. A leasing agreement yields rental income rather than property income to the government. While this may afford a financial incentive for improved performance to the lessor, it may not lead to any greater revenue to the government.

Some developing countries are contemplating or have introduced *debt-equity* swap programmes. Typically, a foreign bank will sell, at a discount, an outstanding loan made to a domestic public sector agency to an investor, most often a multinational company seeking an equity position in the indebted country. The investor presents the loan to the central bank of the indebted country, which will redeem the loan in domestic currency at the prevailing market exchange rate, as long as the investor used the proceeds to acquire a domestic equity interest. In so far as these loans have been guaranteed by the government, such a swap increases the private equity position and reduces the government's external debt burden without drawing on scarce foreign exchange resources.[11]

THE NEW ZEALAND EXPERIENCE: LESSONS FOR IRELAND

There are a number of similarities between the cases of New Zealand and Ireland. Both are small industrial countries, with important agricultural sectors. Both have significant public enterprise sectors in terms of their shares of the total work force employed, in total output and especially in total investment. The activities of state enterprises extend beyond the traditional natural monopolies and include transport, industry, forestry and trade. In both countries the performance of public enterprises in the early part of the 1980s was poor, with low rates of return relative to that in the private sector. In part, this reflects the role of noneeconomic objectives in their operations. Also, through the mid-1980s both countries experienced large fiscal deficits and have been constrained in their fiscal policies by high public debt to GNP ratios.[12]

(1) *Corporatisation and privatisation in New Zealand:* In late 1985 the New Zealand government embarked on a major effort to rationalise and strengthen the operation of its state-owned enterprise (SOE) sector. The goal was to achieve significant improvements in productive and allocative efficiency. Policy interventions were predicated on the belief that such improvements would occur only if the state enterprise sector was more fully exposed to the forces of competition and that enterprise managers operate within a commercial mandate and subject to commercial constraints and adequate financial accountability. Where economies of scale and barriers to entry inhibit the effects of competitive

desired objectives, particularly with respect to personnel decisions (e.g. employment and pay decisions). Pricing decisions were placed in the hands of the SOE managers.

Private sector directors were appointed, making them accountable to shareholding Ministers for the profitable operation of the business. Enterprises were given considerable latitude to discontinue commercially unviable activities unless explicitly funded by the government. For overmanned enterprises, the government had the option of paying the new corporations to employ redundant workers, 'with the costs being booked as social policy costs to the government' or to make direct severance payments to terminated employees (Atkinson, 1988, p. 9).

A number of difficult problems were confronted. The transferral of the businesses required difficult negotiations on an agreed fair market value for the businesses as well as negotiation of appropriate dividend levels and performance targets between the shareholding Ministers and the SOE boards and management. The process was costly, both in terms of external advisory services and in terms of the time required of government officials.

Efforts to deregulate the product market of the SOEs have also been made, thereby 'encouraging cost containment and responsiveness to consumer demand' (New Zealand (a), 101). Equally important has been the effort to increase the exposure of these corporations to competitive pressures. This has essentially required a case by case approach, focusing on the net benefit derived from alternative measures, and taking account of the need to foster adequate incentives and to maintain adequate accountability.

For example, in telecommunications, a timetable for the liberalisation of markets for equipment in customer premises has been established. As of April 1989, all statutory protections of Telecom's monopoly were removed and other firms have been able to provide network services as well; since July, competitors have been allowed to connect with Telecom's own network on 'fair and reasonable' terms. With respect to the electricity corporation, the wholesale generation of electricity was deregulated from the beginning of 1988, with the authorities planning to remove the obligation to supply and the system of area franchising. Prior to the sale of Air New Zealand, main trunk domestic air routes were opened to competing carriers. In other instances (e.g. posts) some statutory restrictions on entry have nevertheless been maintained (OECD, 1989).

Recent reports suggest a significant improvement in productivity in a number of enterprises, with a doubling of output per man in the forestry and coal corporations and major reductions in costs in Electricorp and the postal services. Eight of the nine SOEs were financially profitable in 1988 (despite the need to pay high redundancy payments), though the rates of return on capital are still below that in commercial enterprises. With the exception of the railways, government subsidies have ceased and SOEs paid dividends and taxes equalling NZ$193 million in 1987-8 (OECD, 1989, p. 52). OECD estimates suggest that total government subsidies declined to one-half per cent of GDP by 1988, among the lowest of OECD countries. Thus, the fiscal impact of these measures appears to be positive.

Privatisation emerged as an unintended outgrowth of the corporatisation. The government became aware of the difficulties of persuading the managements of government corporations to act in the interests of shareholders and of monitoring performance in the absence of a market in the corporations' equity. Financial markets were seen as far more adept in monitoring investment decisions, operations performance and financial management as well as a more powerful source of pressure on management to demonstrate a high rate of return on retained earnings (Atkinson, p.5).

In the sale of enterprises, the New Zealand authorities took a different approach from the British. The principal objective remained efficiency improvement, within a regulatory environment conducive to competition. Revenue maximisation was also an important goal. The authorities did not seek to widen share-ownership through the sale of assets at a discount. Moreover, the sale of assets has been accompanied or preceded by actions to foster competition. Sales to a single buyer have been as important as flotation of public shares, in part because a single buyer could more readily introduce structural management reforms, but also because often single buyers have been prepared to pay a premium for acquiring control of the enterprise (OECD,

1989). The government's strategy of privatisation has entailed announcing a list of public assets with combined worth in excess of that amount of the revenue targeted for a given fiscal year, thus allowing the authorities flexibility in negotiating terms with potential buyers. Receipts from the sale of assets have been used to reduce the government's debt.

Sales have included equity in Petrocorp, the Health Computing Services, the Post Office Bank Limited, and Air New Zealand. About a quarter of the Bank of New Zealand is now privately owned. Conditional agreements have been signed for the sale of equity in Maui gas contracts and the Synfuels operations.

(2) *Lessons for Ireland*: The state enterprise sector has long played an important role in the Irish economy. It is now estimated that there are more than 100 state-sponsored bodies (SSB) employing more than twice the number of employees in the civil service and slightly more than are employed in the local and regional bodies (inclusive of the health service) (Barrington, 1985). These employees are in the order of 7 per cent of the total labour force and about 9 per cent of the nonagricultural labour force. Enterprises are distributed throughout the financial, energy, transport and communications, industrial and agricultural sectors.

Commercial state-sponsored bodies exhibited significant financial weakness in the early 1980s. Despite efforts to improve the operations of these bodies, the industrial and transport sectors both showed losses as of 1984. Across firms there was considerable variation in financial results, ranging from firms with high profitability to those requiring longstanding subsidies.

The financial weakness of the state enterprise sector reflected excessive emphasis on the pursuit of noncommercial policy objectives,[14] leading to overstaffing and noneconomic pricing structures (involving intricate cross-subsidisation schemes) and failures in investment design and execution, resulting in large cost overruns and low return on capital. The government at times was forced to inject substantial amounts of equity into a number of public enterprises.

Since 1983, the government has moved to address these problems, and much progress has been made. In 1983 comprehensive and stringent guidelines for the rigorous appraisal of projects were issued. Since 1984, commercial state-sponsored bodies have been required to prepare and annually update five-year corporate plans. These were intended to lead to a consensus between government departments and commercial state-sponsored bodies on their proposed policies, the underlying assumptions and the financial and physical performance targets. Consultation and monitoring between departments and enterprises were intended to ensure that advance discussions occur on any significant policy change. The enterprises were also expected to provide detailed data on their financial operations.[15]

The government also established guidelines for what it considers productive investment — all state-sponsored bodies were expected to aim for a minimum return on capital of 5 per cent. Finally, and of considerable importance, the government substantially reduced the degree of its political interference in SSBs' operations and has encouraged SSBs to focus on profitability. This has led to reduced emphasis on social objectives (and a quantification on the costs of the social and regional objectives imposed on the companies), the elimination of price controls (though some intervention in pricing occasionally occurs) and a willingness to accept cutbacks in employment. These changes are in the same direction as the corporatisation strategy in New Zealand.

The results have been striking. Total employment in the nonfinancial public enterprise sector (NFPE) has fallen by 18 per cent since 1980, from 82,000 to 67,350 in 1987. This reduction is three times the level of decrease in employment in the economy as a whole. Two firms were liquidated (Irish Shipping and Ceimici Teo.). Three new large commercial public enterprises — Bord Telecom, An Post and Coillte — were established. Even more important, the aggregate profitability of the sector switched from net losses of £124 million in 1980 to £50 million in net profits in 1987. Some firms continue to run losses (e.g. B & I, NET, Bord Na Móna, CIE and Irish Steel). Some of these companies are in the process of restructuring, but still pose difficult problems of rationalisation (Sweeney, 1989).

The issue now is how rapidly a privatisation programme should occur. Some privatisation has already begun. Upon liquidation of Irish Shipping, one of its subsidiaries — Irish Continental Lines — was privatised. NET was partly privatised when it sold its assets to IFI, which is now 49 per cent owned by multinational ICI. There is a possibility that the Irish National Petroleum Corporation may be sold to the Nigerian state oil company. However, it would appear that there are a number of state-sponsored bodies where further equity sales would be appropriate, and where the economic or political arguments for state intervention are limited. The pressures of 1992 will further encourage these efforts. Some suggest that state-sponsored bodies engaged in the production of sugar, coal, steel, gas, turf, some trading enterprises and Aer Lingus might be natural candidates. Privatisation may require considerable financial restructuring, particularly in cases where the debt/equity ratio limits the possibility for financial viability.

For many other industries, particularly in situations where there are significant barriers to entry, privatisation may logically follow a period of corporatisation. The process of deregulation implicit in a corporatisation programme may prepare the ground in a number of industries for privatisation.

What are the fiscal arguments for a privatisation scheme? Our earlier analysis raised serious doubts as to whether one can expect significant fiscal gains from privatisation per se in the Irish context. The sale of an enterprise's assets would allow Ireland to reduce its high public debt by the amount of the sale. The amount that can be realised from such sales is likely to be limited, given that present profit levels are not high. Even if there were some improvement in the profit position as a result of privatisation, some informal estimates suggest that a reduction of no more than 5 per cent of the value of the debt would be possible. However, this is not likely to yield a net improvement in the fiscal position of the government if the loss in profit remittances simply offsets the reduction in debt service. This last situation would arise if the sales price of the assets simply equalled the discounted value of the profit stream of the firm.

Several factors could enter to weaken this equivalence.

The perceived value to the budget of the profit remittance stream may be less than that perceived by the private sector, to the extent that the enterprise, while in public hands, may be able to resist full remittance of profits. Differences may exist in the public and private discount rates or in the public and private perception of the probability distribution of profit remittances. In relation to the latter, the vulnerability of the public debt position to explosive growth at current debt levels might imply a higher public valuation of cash-in-hand than is the case for the private sector. Reducing debt through asset sales thus might add to the net worth of the public sector. Finally, to the extent that improved contestability and thus gains in productive efficiency could only emerge from a transfer to private ownership, the government could derive some of the benefit in the value of the sale.

From the perspective of revenue maximisation, the New Zealand strategy of equity sales-cum deregulation would also appear preferable to that observed in the UK. Reliance should be placed on tenders rather than offers for sale, revenue targets should not be predicated on the sale of a small number of enterprises in any given period, and the idea of tranching equity sales so as to allow an initial market valuation of equity should be considered. While minimum priority should be placed on a wide ownership distribution of shares, caution and some regulatory action is likely to be necessary in situations of a monopoly being transferred into the hands of a single private purchaser. Finally, there may be limits on the amount of receipts that can be derived in any one period from equity sales, given the limited size of the Irish equity market.

THE IMPLEMENTATION OF PRIVATISATION

John Williams

Kleinwort Benson

INTRODUCTION

In this paper I would like to offer some general remarks about some of the principal techniques which have been developed in the UK privatisation programme. I will try to concentrate on practical rather than theoretical matters, and to cover subjects which experience indicates are of most interest to those studying privatisation. The four areas I propose to consider are:

(1) *Regulation and competition* – essentially the arrangements which have been developed to prevent privatised concerns from exploiting a monopolistic position after privatisation.
(2) *Relationship with government* – how the privatised company's relationship with the government after privatisation is defined.
(3) *Special shares* – mechanisms for ensuring that the activities of the privatised company cannot conflict with the national interest.
(4) Some of the *practical aspects* of the offer of shares itself, especially the building of demand for the shares and the role of overseas and retail markets.

REGULATION AND COMPETITION

The UK government has privatised a number of monopolies or quasi-monopolies such as BT, British Gas, BAA, and is now preparing for the privatisation of the water and electricity industries. The government has adopted two complementary approaches to constraining the potential for abuse in the dominant market positions of these privatised corporations. The first is to introduce a *regulatory regime*. The second is to introduce *competition*.

The regulatory regime usually has two principal features:
(*a*) a licence which is issued to the privatised corporation. The licence includes a number of terms and conditions designed, for example, to prevent cross-subsidisation within the corporation or to require the provision of specified services. The licence is administered by a regulatory body appointed by the government but whose operations are independent of government;

(*b*) a form of price control, often referred to as the RPI-X formula because it allows the privatised corporation to increase its prices by up to 'x' per cent less than the general level of inflation. This approach to regulation contrasts with the type of regulation typically used in the US. Regulation there focuses on a ceiling on the rate of return on capital rather than on a limit on price increases. The advantages of the RPI-X approach are threefold:

(*i*) it avoids the inherent complication in a return on capital scheme, where definition of profit and calculations of the asset base are difficult to make;

(*ii*) from the the government's point of view, it controls tariffs which are generally considered to be more politically sensitive than profits;

(*iii*) from the investor's point of view, it ensures that efficiency gains flow to investors. There is not the check on the incentive to increase profit which can characterise a rate of return control scheme.

The RPI-X formula was modified in the British Gas and BAA privatisations to reflect the significance to these undertakings of costs in a particular sector rather than movements in the RPI generally. The formula applied is in an RPI-X+Y form. The 'Y' factor allows changes in the specific sector to be reflected in the price ceiling.

The investing market will want to be satisfied that the regulatory regime does not impede the incentive and discipline on management to maximise earnings. The market will also be looking to ensure that the regulatory regime does not give a back door way for interference by the government in the operations of the undertaking.

The second approach to curtailing the potential for abuse of a monopoly position is to introduce *competition* into the sector. I believe the UK government regards regulation as a poor surrogate for competition as a means for encouraging efficient markets.

Increasingly the government is trying to maximise the potential for subjecting privatised companies to competitive pressures. The government, for example, has indicated that it will allow private sector consortia to compete with the restructured state-owned electricity generating companies. The break up of the distribution industry also as part of the privatisation of the electricity industry is another illustration of the introduction of some element of competition.

CONTINUING RELATIONSHIP WITH GOVERNMENT

A clear and binding definition of the relationship between the government and the privatised corporation is critical if investors are to be able to predict with reasonable certainty how the corporation is likely to perform. In particular, potential investors will always look for some reassurance that the government is not able to use any residual shareholding as an instrument of social policy or to exercise any other influence which may detract from the corporation's ability to maximise profits and efficiency. The UK government has always given a binding undertaking to distance itself from the commercial operations of the privatised corporation. This undertaking is set out in the prospectus, normally in the following way:

> HM Government does not intend to use its rights as an ordinary shareholder to intervene in the commercial decisions of the corporation. It does not expect to vote its shareholdings on resolutions moved at General Meetings although it retains the power to do so.

SPECIAL SHARES

A related aspect to the relationship between the government and the privatised corporation is how to establish arrangements which are acceptable to potential investors but will prevent the corporation from acting against the public interest. For example, the government has been keen in a number of privatisations to ensure that the privatised corporations cannot be owned or become effectively controlled by non-UK parties without the government's consent. The mechanism which has been developed to prevent such an unwelcome takeover is known as the golden or special share.

The special share typically operates in the following way. The government requires the corporation to include in its Articles of Association a provision that no person can own more than 15 per cent of the corporation's share capital. The corporation also issues to the government a special share with special voting rights which are triggered only if an amendment to the relevant Article is proposed. These voting rights once triggered will allow the government to out-vote all other shareholders.

The principal benefit of this mechanism from the investor's perspective is that the voting rights attached to the special share can only be triggered in well-defined circumstances and only in response to those circumstances. It is essentially a passive instrument which cannot be used by the government to interfere in the day-to-day operations of the corporation.

COMPETITIVE SCARCITY

At the core of any privatisation is a flotation or share sale. The technical aspects of these transactions are broadly similar whether it is a flotation or share sale by the government or a private sector company. In other words, a prospectus must be prepared, an accountant's report must be undertaken, capital reorganisations must be implemented and so on. A privatisation is not an unusual transaction in that sense. How is it different?

One distinguishing feature of most privatisations is their size in relation to other more conventional equity issues. Privatisations will often exceed by several times the size of familiar, private sector equity offers. A second distinguishing feature is the political setting of a privatisation. A privatisation is a political, as much as a financial, exercise. In the UK the government typically sets the following objectives for any privatisation:

(*i*) to broaden and deepen share ownership;

(*ii*) to maximise the proceeds from the flotation;
(*iii*) to maximise competition within the industry.

There are tensions between these objectives. Maximising proceeds can conflict with maximising share ownership. A bought deal or auction to professional investors might in some circumstances increase proceeds but would do nothing for the spread of share ownership. There can also be tension between maximising proceeds and maximising competition. Investors are likely to be prepared to pay more for a monopoly than for an undertaking whose financial performance will depend on unpredictable competitive pressures. Furthermore, the government is not a single client. It is composed of Ministers and civil servants whose perspectives can be different. It is also composed of a series of individual departments whose perspectives and objectives will also differ. In the 1984 privatisation of BT, the following government departments had an involvement:

> Department of Trade and Industry
> HM Treasury
> Bank of England
> Foreign and Commonwealth Office
> Home Office
> Ministry of Defence
> No 10 Policy Unit
> Cabinet Office

A key task which faces governments and advisers in this setting is how to reconcile the government's objectives and to develop sufficient demand to ensure that the offer on such a scale is taken up at an acceptable price.

The approach in the UK has been to try to achieve the widest appeal in not simply the institutional market but also among the general public and in overseas markets. The experience in the UK has been that powerful, competitive dynamics can develop between these separate markets. A sense of scarcity develops which, depending on the structure of the offer, can build and so create the capacity successfully to absorb substantial equity issues.

The equity market crash of October 1987 and the consequences of the BP share sale raise questions about the continuing viability of this strategy and whether there will be sufficient demand for equity in each of the markets to generate the competitive scarcity effect. I am generally positive about the prospects — certainly in the UK:

(*a*) the *institutional* market appears to be redeveloping its appetite for equity. It is likely to be attracted to equity offers which demonstrate the type of high-quality earnings typical of most privatisation issues;

(*b*) the *retail* market has been a major source of demand for privatisation issues in the UK. The policy of broadening and deepening share ownership may have been knocked by the BP share offer, and the increase in inflows to building societies seems to reflect something of a flight to safety. The building societies themselves may, ironically, play an important role in re-establishing the retail sector's confidence in equities. A number of building societies are currently contemplating conversion to plc status. As part of the conversion process, societies may — as Abbey National is now proposing — offer shares on a preferential basis or distribute free shares to their members. Such distributions, which could involve several million individuals, could help to rebuild the confidence of the retail sector in equities and bring a new vitality to the government's wider share ownership policies;

(*c*) the *overseas* market seems less certain following the BP sale. The difficulties with the overseas tranches, particularly in the US, appeared to arise largely because the lead managers did not reduce the risk they were carrying by using larger underwriting groups. The difficulties did not seem to arise through any particular weakness among overseas investors.

PRIVATISATION
AND THE IRISH FINANCIAL SECTOR

Philip J. Kelly

Cooney, Corrigan & Kelly

INTRODUCTION

On a narrow construction of the title, this paper would look at the prospects for and implications of moves to privatise state-owned financial institutions in Ireland. A somewhat broader view could assess the impact and opportunities of privatisation measures — adopted in different sectors — for financial institutions, be they state owned or in the private sector. However, for reasons which I outline in the paper, the prospects for widescale privatisation of state-owned enterprises in Ireland are limited in the near future. As I also believe there is merit in viewing privatisation as only one form of changing ownership, it is on this latter dimension of ownership structures and the conduct and performance of enterprises in terms of economic efficiency that I concentrate.

As definitions of privatisation, and the arguments advanced both in its favour and against, have already been covered in other papers, I do not propose to cover these aspects. Privatisation is taken here to refer to sales of state enterprises as it is this form that is most relevant to financial institutions. Reduced state involvement through contracting out of services, sales of local authority houses etc., are not therefore included. Instead the paper begins by examining privatisation in the Irish context. It is argued that for various practical, traditional and political reasons, widescale privatisation is not likely in the near future. The paper then goes on to outline the interaction between ownership, conduct, performance, competition and efficiency. The next section concludes that the financial sector in Ireland should focus on changing ownership structures within the sector and in other sectors in Ireland, as well as EC and international developments, which will have a far greater impact than privatisation of state enterprises in Ireland.

PRIVATISATION IN AN IRISH CONTEXT

When looking at the privatisation issue in an Irish context, it is worth noting the extent to which direct state involvement has been favoured in so many areas. In the financial sector there are Irish Life, ICC (Industrial Credit Corporation), ACC (Agricultural Credit Corporation), HFA (Housing Finance Agency), Post Office Savings Bank, Prize Bonds, National Lottery and a hybrid form of state involvement in more recent years through the administration of ICI (Insurance Corporation of Ireland) and PMPA. In other spheres such as so-called 'natural monopolies', where it was thought that duplication of investment in facilities such as electricity and railways would be wasteful, Ireland also has direct state involvement. In manufacturing, transport and communications there are state enterprises such as Irish Sugar Company, Aer Lingus (airline), Aer Rianta (airports), Telecom Eireann, etc.

The circumstances in which many of these enterprises arose have varied considerably. Some, such as the ESB (Electricity Supply Board), were set up as new bodies from the beginning. Others, such as CIE and its successors Dublin Bus, Irish Rail, Irish Bus, emerged from a rationalisation of private firms. There are also examples of state bodies emerging because of particular circumstances at a particular time, such as Dublin Gas and the Irish National Petroleum Corporation (INPC), which later encompassed Irish Refining Ltd at Whitegate and Bantry Terminals at Whiddy Island.

Hence the rationale behind state involvement in enterprises has varied dramatically. Indeed, in many cases the rationale for the establishment of enterprises as state bodies no longer exists to the same degree. Yet, there is no a consistent approach to state involvement — the course of action in tackling particular situations is reactive rather than strategically chosen. For example, in recent years Dublin Gas moved into the state sector, Irish Shipping was closed, Foir

Teo has been closed, NET (fertiliser manufacturer) entered into a joint venture with a private sector multinational to become IFI, Irish Steel is proposed to be sold direct to another steel company.

Meanwhile new state organisations are being set up including Bord Glas (The Horticulture Board) and Bord Coillte (The Forestry Board). In many cases, a wholly pragmatic approach is taken, which revolves around short-term solutions to particular situations.

To date there has been little real discussion on whether privatisation is a policy that should be pursued, which are the most appropriate candidates for privatisation should it be chosen, or the form of privatisation that should be adopted.

In some senses, the opposition in principle to selling state assets in certain quarters such as trade unions, means the issued is not highlighted for fear of causing difficulties in getting cooperation on other aspects of government economic policy, including national understandings on wage increases.

In Ireland the most appealing candidate for privatisation is in the financial sector, namely Irish Life. This is mainly due to the fact that politically it is appealing as it may generate substantial once-off revenue to the government. However, there are particular legal difficulties in establishing whether it is the shareholder (mainly the Minister for Finance) or the with-profits policy holder who is entitled to the reserves in Irish Life. If it is the policy holder that is deemed to be entitled to the reserves, the windfall to government from the sale of Irish Life could be considerably reduced.

The second aspect of Irish Life's proposed sale is that it could be portrayed as being a necessary step to allow expansion into certain US states where there may be difficulties in operating as a state-owned enterprise. In other words, the government can state that it needs to reduce its shareholding in Irish Life in order to get over a legal difficulty impeding its expansion. Thirdly, there is now no compelling reason for the state to be involved in this sector, and generally privatisation takes place first of all in enterprises which face significant competition from the private sector. It must be said, however, that Irish Life was itself originally established through the rationalisation of private sector firms.

Fourthly, management and staff at Irish Life probably see themselves more closely aligned with the private sector than with other state-owned/controlled enterprises. Irish Life is also an enterprise unlikely to provoke the type of opposition to privatisation that view it purely as 'Thatcherite policy' and almost because of that alone one which should not be adopted. This example has sufficient unique dimensions to persuade me that it might well be a once-off case of privatisation. It remains to be seen whether the privatisation of what would be viewed as more mainstream enterprises such as the ESB, Aer Rianta etc. would face as little debate/opposition as the deliberations on Irish Life. For example, it is difficult to see private sector water authorities being established in Ireland in the near future, and getting paid for their services, given the recent experience with the introduction of water charges by local authorities some years ago and the failure of the charges to be collected.

As well as change in ownership from public to private institutions and individuals, in Ireland's case, because of the small size of economy, there is also the strong possibility that under privatisation, nationality of ownership would change. Whether this would be a deterring factor remains to be seen. It could be of political and psychological significance, if not of real economic significance, given that nationality of ownership was itself a factor responsible for setting up certain state bodies, e.g. INPC.

While the holding of a golden share which would allow the government to outvote other shareholders on matters of vital national interest could play a part in this respect, the prospect of changing nationality of ownership could further delay, if not disrupt, moves towards privatisation.

A feature of the privatisation programme undertaken in the UK has been the time-lag between the proposals first being put forward and then being carried out. This is especially true of the placing of shares and the offer of shares for sale as opposed to direct sales of assets as in the proposals on Irish Steel. The parliamentary time taken up in adopting the legislative changes for the privatisation of statutory bodies has been long in the UK. If that were to be repeated in Ireland it would require that a government going along such a route would need to be committed in principle as well as on pragmatic grounds to the idea. Secondly, the number of privatisations would be low and the timescale long. Of course, this would have benefits in terms of not crowding funding requirements into a short timescale.

Apart from parliamentary time and the preparation of legislation, in some cases, to permit privatisation, there will often be a time-lag needed to allow a build-up of the state enterprises balance sheet. This may involve write-off of debt or injections of long promised and often postponed funds by government. Underwriting arrangements and flotations also take time to prepare and implement and, in certain cases, regulatory agencies might need to be set up to oversee performance following privatisation.

In the context of the delays in getting privatisation off the ground it is worth bearing in mind that the wider economic, political and social environment to which Ireland is exposed may be changing. The 1980s has been an era of drawing back the state and promoting the workings of markets in many countries.

The 1990s may see some changes in this respect, as left-wing parties begin to assert themselves once again in Britain and in Europe. While left-wing parties may no longer view state ownership and direct state involvement as the ultimate economic objective, (indeed in many countries, such parties have themselves initiated privatisation measures), there could still be less of an impetus for privatisation than existed in the 1980s.

In Ireland, where debate or discussion on privatisation on grounds of principle rather than on grounds of pragmatism has not taken place, changes in the sea of public opinion, especially in Western Europe and the UK, could quickly quell what might in any event be controversial moves to privatise state assets.

The foregoing discussion of issues surrounding privatisation in Ireland illustrates the grounds for my belief that there is little prospect of a widespread privatisation programme in the immediate future. For that reason, and also because I believe that privatisation should be seen as only one form of change in ownership structure to which enterprises are exposed, this paper goes on to discuss the relationship between enterprises, their financing, ownership, conduct and performance.

OWNERSHIP, CONDUCT & PERFORMANCE, EFFICIENCY
From the point of view of the economy, we should be primarily interested in forms of ownership because of economic efficiency arguments. Which form of ownership produces the right goods efficiently at a minimum cost? The arguments advanced here are that it is management of the resources more than ownership that counts most. The constraints on poor management derive from competition and the form of regulatory environment which ensures competition rather than ownership per se.

In the private sector the threat of replacement through recruitment or takeover places a discipline on incumbent management. Ownership on its own, because of the divorce of ownership from management control in most enterprises, is not sufficient to give this discipline. It is competition which throws up inter-firm comparisons, which allows assessments of the management and firm's relative performance, where owners do not have the same volume of information as management. While to some extent the growing role of institutional shareholders puts performance under more professional scrutiny than that provided by individual shareholders, lack of specific industry knowledge and experience means that analysts rely heavily on inter-firm comparisons.

In the public sector there are added difficulties for 'owners' in the sense of the general public seeking to assess performance. Sometimes governments themselves do no want the public to know the true performance of firms, as they may have forced the firm to fulfil objectives other than those for which it has been established or because of public embarrassment at the failure of past policy decisions. Also, the public have little incentive to monitor performance and little effective sanctions against poor management performance.

In the public sector there is another significant difficulty in that the 'control' exerted by civil servants on management in the interest of preventing foul-ups which will embarrass Ministers, are exactly the type of controls that cause time-lags and missed opportunities, which are clots in the life blood of commercial activity. In other words, while the private sector has a divorce of ownership from management control, the public sector has yet another layer which gives ownership to the general public through their elected representatives in government, control to civil servants and a constrained form of management to those in the day-to-day running of the enterprise.

In my opinion, the policy of government towards state enterprises, as operated by civil servants, is probably a more significant form of weakness in the state enterprise system than state ownership itself. In these circumstances it is little wonder that, judged on the performance criteria applied to the private sector generally, public sector enterprises do not always shine.

This comparative approach also ignores, however, the fact that such comparisons may not be valid, in that the state enterprises may be in existence to achieve non-commercial objectives unlikely to be aimed at by firms in the private sector.

Ownership on its own does not determine conduct and performance because of the extent to which management of larger, private enterprises are in control. In the public sector the further layer of control rests often with the state's bureaucracy, driving yet another wedge between ownership, control and performance. This question of the effect of ownership on performance has been borne out by studies of the relative performance of public and private enterprises following changes in the nature of their ownership; these have been inconclusive in their findings as reported in other papers given here. Given that what we seek is economic efficiency, one needs to consider the role of competition in encouraging efficiency and how competition should be ensured.

In doing so is it important to bear in mind that market forces do not guarantee competition in all cases — indeed, actors in the market place often seek to eradicate competitive forces. For example, concern exists that even with privatisation of state enterprises, market forces may not be sufficient to generate competition and one could end up with a private monopoly or cartel arrangement replacing a public monopoly. Thus the motivation behind setting up regulatory agencies to control such privatised firms, after they have been taken out of the state sector.

In recent years, regulation of markets in a minimalist way has been the direction most favoured by governments in Western Europe seeking to intervene in the marketplace to achieve certain objectives which the market itself is failing to achieve. The regulation of structures (e.g. controlling monopolies and mergers) the regulation of conduct through fair trade inquiries and analysis of performance by regulatory agencies as well as predators and suitors, all serve as constraints on enterprises, and should act as supports to competition and efficiency. This whole area is one which has been neglected in Ireland and which has received prominence only in response to specific situations. Examples include pressure for investigations arising from falls in bread prices, increases in fuel prices or curiosity and concern regarding the ownership of companies which have remained anonymous, as in the case of the meat industry.

Competition is prima facie presumed to exist in Ireland and only the anomalies are thought to need investigating. Given the small size of the country, the extent of interlocking arrangements between business, both in and between sectors, and the personal relationships which exist across many businesses, it would be remarkable if competitive forces in Ireland were as strong as in the more anonymous workings of larger markets. For this reason, competition policy in Ireland should involve more than passively waiting for suspicions of non-competitive behaviour. This is not to advocate increased regulation and intervention for its own sake, but rather to ensure the need for an active competition policy to seek free access and exit to and from sectors rather than relying solely on regulating behaviour within sectors.

To sum up this section, it is pointed out that ownership is less important than competition as an encouragement of efficiency. Secondly, market forces on their own do not guarantee competition. For these reasons more attention needs to be placed in policy circles on how competition can be encouraged and ensured as a means of improving performance and efficiency without introducing an overregulated environment.

CHANGING OWNERSHIP AND THE FINANCIAL SECTOR
The financial sector in Ireland comprises banks, life insurance

companies, pension funds, building societies, credit unions, finance companies and financial advisory bodies. The changes in the financial sector internationally and the additional changes arising from integration of the European market are accentuating the pressures for change within the sector in Ireland. As the regulatory environment and tax system begin to treat the different elements in the financial sector in a similar fashion, there will be implications for the way the main financial services are provided to the personal, corporate and government sectors of the market.

Changing ownership structures are occurring on a wide scale over all sectors, internationally and in Ireland.

Management buy-outs, leveraged buy-outs, the takeovers of agricultural cooperatives by companies, the demutualisation of building societies, the conversion of entities such as trustee savings banks to companies, mergers and takeovers, including those of a transnational nature, all put the issue of ownership into a fluid state. Furthermore, with steps towards integration of markets in Europe and with moves to liberalise market sectors including the financial sector, the focus of attention is rightly shifting from ownership to conduct and performance by enterprises. All of these changing ownership structures are providing opportunities for firms in the financial sector.

They also raise issues relating to property rights. For example, is it valid in a management buy-out for the existing management, who after all are running an enterprise on behalf of the shareholders, to offer to buy the company from existing shareholders, on the expectation that they can improve performance under their own ownership? Should some form of protection for shareholders and for competing bidders not be established to ensure that the interests of all are served, in a situation where one presumes that management has greater access to information and knowledge of the firm than either shareholders or competing bidders?

An example in the financial sector of possible changes in property rights arises with building societies, where it is now possible under the Building Societies Act 1988 to convert from a mutual body to a company. The mutual form of organisation, whereby depositors with the Society are deemed to be members, limits the capital available to societies to the reserves that have accrued. Of course, some will argue that the philosophical basis which lay behind the origins of the cooperative and building society movements is being abandoned for profits in moving from a mutual to a company status. In the integrated and competing financial markets that are now aimed at it is difficult to segment the market in the same way as in the past. All institutions are beginning to compete for funds between different uses.

Building societies are transferring from almost complete concentration on house purchase to personal lending. Banks are moving into the house purchase market as well as having a diversified lending base in the personal and commercial sectors. The building societies are limited in their diversification by a lack of long-term capital resources as they do not have the possibility of issuing equity in order to raise capital.

Under the Building Societies Act, 1988, building societies have the right to engage in a wider range of activities. It is argued that many of the societies will be able to do this within their present structure. However, it is likely that changes will take place such as amalgamations of societies and, in the longer term, conversion to company status. This latter move may often be a defensive reaction towards takeover efforts by companies such as banks. The Building Societies Act, 1988 provides a five-year protection period for building societies which convert from mutual to company status. The sanctuary that this five-year period offers may well appeal to managers/directors of building societies, on the basis that it gives them a breathing period in which they can seek out desirable partners rather than be obliged to join forces with less desirable partners because of changing market circumstances. However, there are issues as to who should benefit from changes to company status. Is it valid that members of two years' standing should become shareholders in the new entity? What about past depositors who helped build up the reserves?

In South Africa and Australia, where the legislative capacity to change from a mutual body to a company has been in existence for some years, most societies have converted their status. In the UK, where the capacity to convert to a company has been available since the Building Societies Act, 1986, the option of conversion has been taken by one major society. The scale of building societies today is far greater than was envisaged when the mutual form of organisation was first adopted. The diverse form of ownership of large mutual bodies has put managers/directors in a far greater position of power than would be available to a publicly quoted company, which is always subject to threat of takeover.

A further example of changing ownership structure revolves around the change away from the direct provision of banking loans to the commercial sector towards securitisation of investment in industry and the raising of capital in equity markets. In line with trends internationally, external funds for non-financial firms in Ireland will increasingly be obtained from non-bank savings collection institutions such as pension funds, life assurance companies, etc. Banks and other deposit-taking institutions, such as building societies, will operate more in the personal sector and will rely on funds raised in credit markets. This change in the nature of ownership and control of non-financial firms by institutional investors is of greater significance to the development of the Irish financial sector than the impact of privatisation is likely to be. It is also of direct relevance to the performance of the non-financial sector, given that the criteria that institutional investors might apply could place a greater emphasis on short-term results over long-term business strategies.

In the context of the rapid changes taking place internationally in financial markets it is essential that the regulatory environment and the tax environment facing financial institutions remove many of the anomalies and discriminatory treatment of different segments of the financial sector. Only by ensuring efficiency in the operation of the financial markets, and active competition and transparency in the operation of capital and credit markets, can we be sure that not only the financial sector but also the non-financial sector in Ireland is in a position to take account of the internationalisation of business and of finance. In general, however, attention should be focused on the promotion of competition and examinations of conduct and performance rather than confining discussion to the issue of ownership. In these respects, in Ireland, privatisation as an issue pales into insignificance relative to the other changes that need to occur.

PRIVATISATION
AND SOCIAL INSURANCE

John Blackwell

University College, Dublin

INTRODUCTION

This paper on privatisation and social security begins by
setting the system of social security in context. It then
considers some of the ways in which privatisation occurs in
social security and the rationale for this. There follows a brief
analysis of some of the key issues, putting the Irish
experience where possible in an international context.

THE SCOPE OF SOCIAL SECURITY

By social security we mean programmes established by
government which insure individuals against interruption or
loss of earning power and certain special expenditures which
arise, such as from ill-health. Allowances to families for the
maintenance of children are included in this definition. In
turn, protection of people and their dependants can be
ensured either through cash payments or in the form of
resources such as hospital and medical care and rehabili-
tation. The cash benefits can be termed income maintenance
programmes, while the programmes which finance or provide
direct services to people can be termed benefits in kind.

In turn, under income maintenance programmes, there
are three broad approaches which are observable across
different countries. First, there are employment-related
systems. Here, the eligibility for pensions (for example) and
other payments are based directly or indirectly on the length
of the period spent in employment; and the level of benefit is
usually linked to the level of the earnings of the worker

before old age, unemployment, sickness or whatever other contingency caused these earnings to cease. These programmes are financed mainly or entirely by contributions of employers and workers, usually as a proportion of earnings. These could be termed social insurance programmes. Across countries, governments participate in the financing of these programmes, for instance by covering all or part of the costs of programmes or by paying a subsidy in order to cover any deficit in an insurance fund.

Second, there are universal programmes, which provide flat-rate cash benefits to people without respect to income, means or employment. These are usually financed from general Exchequer revenues. An example in Ireland would be Child Benefit, paid on a universal basis for children up to the ages of 16-17.

Third, there are means-tested programmes, where eligibility for benefits is assessed by testing the resources of the individuals or the family against a standard which is often close to the subsistence level. Benefits are limited to these needy or low-income applicants. There may be an effective marginal tax rate as earnings from work whereby, for every unit of earnings from work, a certain proportion of that is lost in reduced means-tested benefits. These benefits are financed mainly from the general revenue of the Exchequer. These 'social assistance' programmes are welfare programmes in the broadest sense. An example in Ireland would the Supplementary Welfare Allowance, which is supposed to play the role of providing a minimal level of income below which no person (as long as they are not working for 30 or more hours a week) should fall.

It might be argued that social assistance-type programmes should be excluded from the remit of this paper, given the differences between them and social insurance, both in regard to coverage and methods of financing. However, there is in fact a spectrum of benefits ranging from social insurance to social assistance, with a grey area between these types of benefit. Moreover, social insurance is not insurance in the classic sense of the term, as the benefits are not funded, there is part-financing by the state and contribution rates are not risk related. Hence, the spectrum of social security is covered in this paper, although the issues about direct provision of health services — specifically about choices between public production of health services and private production — are not covered.

A wide range of risks is covered by social security, ranging from unemployment to invalidity, employment injuries and occupational diseases, maternity and sickness; in addition there is coverage for old age and there are family benefits. In Ireland the state provides social security through a combination of insurance-based benefits (whereby contributory benefits are received if people have built up a sufficient record of contributions) and assistance. In the latter case, assistance payments are made on a means-tested basis. As well as direct provision, the state engages in subsidisation. In particular, relief is allowed for income tax purposes for medical insurance premiums. Up to recent years, the state has been less in evidence in regulating private provisions (e.g. of occupational pensions).

By comparison with other European countries, there is less reliance on income-related benefits in Ireland. Moreover, there is a heavier reliance in Ireland on covering the additional costs of children through the child dependent allowances which are an integral part of the social security system. By contrast, in many other European countries, there are relatively generous family allowances which are paid whether or not the recipients are in receipt of contingent benefits.

For 1987, it can be estimated that means-tested benefits comprise some £560 million out of the total of £1320 million of family income support, unemployment compensation and Child Benefit. In the same year about 30 per cent of the population (adults together with their dependants) would have been depending on the social welfare system for most or all of their household income.

CHANGE IN SOCIAL SECURITY OVER TIME
In Ireland as in many other OECD countries, the social security programme is the largest single item of government expenditure, as well as one of the items which has grown fastest over time. Between 1980 and 1986, current transfer payments on social security and welfare increased from 10.6 per cent of GNP to 15.7 per cent of GNP.

The growth of social expenditure over time in Ireland has been much influenced by the marked increase in unemployment in the period 1980-87. By 1985, public expenditure on unemployment as a percentage of Gross Domestic Product, 3.6 per cent, was higher than in any other OECD country (OECD, 1988, Table 3). If the expenditure data were expressed as a percentage of Gross National Product, Ireland would show up even higher in relative terms, since GNP is less than GDP in Ireland. Unemployment compensation (£681 million) and old-age benefits (£690.7 million) head the list of social protection benefits in 1987 (Central Statistics Office, 1989), with sickness benefits third at £344 million.

AIMS OF SOCIAL SECURITY

Before the rationale for privatisation in social security is presented, it is worth noting that systems of social security are trying to do a number of different things:

(*a*) to provide a minimum income guarantee or safety net, below which households should not fall; linked to this (although in principle a separate aim) is the redistribution of household income towards those at the bottom of the income distribution, away from those at the top;

(*b*) to replace some proportion of the income from work which is lost due to specific contingencies such as old age, unemployment and sickness;

(*c*) to give family income support which relates to the child-rearing period and to the care which is given within the household to elderly or disabled relatives;

(*d*) to share equitably between people the financial costs of these systems.

From the point of view of any one period, social protection involves income transfers to particular households, funded by taxation levied (largely) on those who are at work. By contrast, from the viewpoint of the life cycle, some social protection involves support for elderly people (who may or may not have been disadvantaged during their working careers), and support which is related to particular tasks such as child rearing and caring.

PRIVATISATION IN SOCIAL SECURITY

In social security, one can define privatisation as an increase in the relative role of private production or private finance in any of the activities which are outlined above. It means effectively a tendency to limit the protection given by the public system of social security, possibly reducing it to the role of basic protection, and completing it by private arrangements, both collective and individual. These private arrangements can be facilitated by tax concessions.

Such a definition of privatisation would in some ways be inappropriate for social security, because for most people the bulk of their income comes from the labour market. Hence, the role of the market can change due to elements which have nothing to do with privatisation — for instance, due to changes in unemployment. In this regard, it is relevant that between 1979 and 1987 the real income after direct taxes (income taxes and employee social insurance contributions) of a married worker with one spouse earning an average industrial wage (transportable goods industries, males on adult rates of pay) fell by 9.1 per cent.

Alternatively, one can use a threefold division of state involvement in economic and social activity (Le Grand and Robinson, 1984): direct provision, subsidy and regulations. In the case of social security, the commodities which are 'produced' are insurance and redistribution. In parallel with this classification, privatisation can involve reductions in the role of the state under any of these headings.

FORMS OF PRIVATISATION
The main ways in which privatisation can occur in social security are where private insurance against contingencies such as sickness and pensions is made compulsory and where governments require third parties, typically employers, to organise or provide income security. Governments could use legislation or regulation in order to ensure that employers provide the coverage.

To some extent, reductions in relative levels of benefit and restrictions in coverage of benefits such as have occurred in a number of OECD countries, though not to any marked extent to date in Ireland, are themselves forms of privatisation, if only of an indirect nature. Not only is the role of government reduced in these cases but also such withdrawal is likely to result in individuals purchasing more private insurance (that is, in cases where markets exist, as in the case of pension provision).

Such a withdrawal on the part of the state could have significant impacts on the distribution of income. This is because, both for Ireland and for other OECD countries, the system of cash benefits is, on balance, highly redistributive towards lower income groups (Rottman and Reidy, 1988; O'Higgins, 1985; Saunders, 1984; Danziger *et al.*, 1981; Sawyer, 1982), with in-kind services such as national health being marginally egalitarian in their impacts. Hence, if welfare privatisation took the form of a relative reduced role for the state by comparison with the market, with the relative impacts on income distribution within each form being unchanged, it would push the income distribution in a more unequal direction.

RATIONALE FOR PRIVATISATION

Aside from the 'pragmatic' argument which arises from the objective of cutting public expenditure (either as a prelude to lower rates of direct taxation or in order to reduce the national debt), the economic arguments for privatisation are usually, first, that the private sector will produce any commodity more efficiently than the public sector because of the operation of market forces, and second, that the output produced in quantity and quality will be more in tune with the wishes of the consumer than is the case with public production.

If social insurance is viewed simply as private insurance which is run by the state, it might indeed by maintained that it could be run more efficiently as a private operation. However, there are some respects in which social insurance differs in character from private insurance. First, social insurance does not provide an actuarially fair return to each person. This reflects the fact that benefits do not match contributions. In turn, this can reflect the use of social insurance for purposes of redistribution. It is possible for governments to vary the relationship between benefits and contributions in order to benefit lower paid workers. Furthermore, as discussed in Atkinson (1986) while private insurance policies are rather tightly drawn, specifying contingencies and benefits which cannot in general be varied, a social insurance scheme has more flexibility. The government may vary the terms over time, especially in order to cover needs which were not envisaged earlier on.

Second, social insurance does not involve funding. In turn, this reflects the ability of governments to compel successive generations of citizens to be insured and the ability to tax under a pay-as-you-go system.

Third, a good deal of private insurance consists of group insurance. This is observed, for instance, in the case of occupational pensions.

Would one expect that private insurance would be more efficient than social insurance? There are a number of different issues here. First, would private companies be better organised and have lower administrative costs than the public equivalents? This depends in part on whether public insurance could reap advantages of economies of scale by comparison with the existence of a number of private companies.

Second, it could be argued that a private system has the advantage of offering a choice between different suppliers of insurance. This argument about the gains from diversity of choice depends on the extent to which people differ in their attitude to risk (Atkinson, 1986). Private insurance would allow some people to opt out of the current public insurance for all.

There is another type of diversity: that one could choose from a number of private suppliers of insurance. There is, however, no presumption that private provision would *inherently* be more efficient than public provision. Suppose that different individuals are in different risk groups and know to which group they belong but that the insurance company cannot identify the riskiness of an individual. If the insurance company sets premiums according to the average risk, this premium will be regarded as being extremely high for those with low risks. As a result, the insurer will be left with the relatively high-risk cases being insured at a rate which is actuarially set too low. In the insurance literature, this is the case of adverse selection. Insurance companies can try to overcome the problem by asking potential customers to disclose relevant facts.

Third, it is not clear that private arrangements would be more efficient than public ones in terms of their coverage of different groups. Private schemes could be tempted to restrict coverage to particular segments of the labour force.

Hence, using efficiency criteria, the choice between private and public insurance is not clear — it depends on empirical issues such as cost of provision under different systems.

Even if private provision were found to be more efficient than public, the public interventions could still be justified in terms of income distribution. This will be taken up later, using the case of health insurance.

There is a separate strand of arguments about the inefficiency of the welfare state: that the social security system dampens the incentives to work and to save. The argument about work is that cash transfers induce people to quit work and to spend a longer period of time unemployed. A survey of the evidence on the extent to which unemployment has been induced by social security transfers (Blackwell, 1986) suggests that, while there may have been some impact on unemployment duration, it is unlikely to have been large. It should be noted that the arguments here are not about replacing public by private provision but about a 'pure' reduction in public provision. The case of disability benefits is considered below. Most of the work on the impact of social security on savings is for the US: the estimates are that private savings are towards the lower end of a range 0-20 per cent lower than they would be in the absence of social security (Danziger *et al.*, 1981).

There is another incentive effect: the so-called 'poverty trap' whereby the operations of both means-tested social security benefits and means-tested social services can lead to someone who increases his or her hours of work to lose more in terms of loss of benefits and increases in direct taxes than the increase in gross pay. While there can be marked poverty traps in Ireland (Blackwell, 1988), the remedy lies not in privatisation but in structural reform of cash benefits and a greater degree of coherence between social security benefits and direct taxes.

POLICIES ADOPTED

In a number of European countries in recent years, the proposals — some of them adopted, at least to some degree — for reducing the involvement of the state in social security have been of two broad types. First, there has been a proposed move towards means-tested benefits, on grounds that as a result the benefits would be more closely directed towards those who are in need, thereby achieving a greater degree of cost effectiveness. Second, there have been proposals to replace social insurance in part at least by private insurance.

Since the late 1970s, many countries have altered the structure and rates of payment of social security in ways which have meant less generous benefits and tighter conditions necessary to qualify. In many cases this has happened in the countries with the most highly developed welfare states. This is not uniformly the case, as the US has seen a number of such policy changes.

These policy moves have in a number of instances been a reaction to budgetary pressures. In particular, in the case of pensions they have reflected imminent or longer run difficulties in financing social security pensions. By contrast, policy changes in the UK and the US have been aimed at reducing the perceived disincentive effects of social security benefits.

The main moves towards privatisation in other European countries have involved pensions and sick pay. Pay-related pensions are typically financed on a pay-as-you-go basis, with taxes on the current generation at work financing benefits for the currently retired generation. This 'social contract' between successive generations can persist in harmony as long as major changes do not occur in the sizes of the respective generations. With the pronounced ageing of the population which is in prospect in many OECD countries, although not in Ireland, this social contract is coming under strain. Between 1986 and 2020 the proportion of the population aged 65 and over in the OECD area as a whole is projected to increase from 12.7 per cent to 18 per cent.

Occupational pension schemes play an important role in supplementing public schemes across OECD countries — even in cases where earnings-related pensions are available under social security (such as the UK, the US and the Netherlands). In recent years, Switzerland has made a supplementary occupational pension scheme mandatory.

In the UK the state earnings-related pensions scheme has been scaled down. This measure has been complemented by incentives which have been given to people to take out private pensions, including a rebate on contributions and allowing people to take out personal pensions as an alternative to either state or employer schemes. It is worth noting that this means that individual employers and employees now bear more of the risks (regarding the returns on investments) than was the case in the past.

Also in the UK, certain social security benefits have been transferred to employers with the introduction of statutory sick pay, under which employers are responsible for sick pay for the first 28 weeks, the cost being deductible against their social security contributions. This has now been extended to maternity pay.

THE DEBATE IN IRELAND

By contrast with other EEC countries, there has not been much public debate, or debate at political level about privatisation in matters of social security. This partly reflects the fact that the welfare state in Ireland is less developed than in many other European countries. It also reflects the fact that a considerable number of persons in employment are self employed (including a relatively high proportion in agriculture) and up to recent years were not covered by existing social insurance provisions. Hence, some of the policy debate in recent years has been about the extent to which, and the terms under which, state protection should be extended to these people who do not have coverage at the moment.

The two main areas in which there has effectively been a policy debate in recent years about privatisation have been pensions and disability benefit. These are now taken up in turn.

Pensions: For many years in Ireland the state has encouraged the setting up of private occupational pension schemes by giving relief from income tax on contributions paid under approved schemes by employers and employees and on the income of these schemes from investment and deposits. Currently, social security pensions cover all employees but the benefits are not related to earnings. By contrast, occupational pensions are usually related to earnings. There is no compulsion on firms to provide occupational pensions for their workers. However, such schemes have grown over time. By 1978, coverage of occupational schemes in the public sector had reached 85 per cent but was much less in the private sector. By the mid-1980s, some 50 per cent of employees were members of company pension schemes (public and private sectors combined). This figure showed little change from the coverage of the late 1970s and reflected in part the impact of the recession in the Irish economy in the period 1979-85. A survey for 1985 shows 47 per cent of the employed labour force covered, compared with 45 per cent for 1976 (Commission on Social Welfare, 1986). Currently, some 60 per cent of employees are covered by occupational pension schemes, with marked differences being observed in the nature of benefits (such as whether flat-rate, proportion of final earnings) across such schemes.

A major factor contributing to the development of private schemes in Ireland as in most countries has been that the typical state scheme has taken inadequate account of the fact that people do not want to experience too dramatic a decline in income when they retire. The main advantage offered by private schemes has been their ability to provide income-related pensions not subject to arbitrary maxima. The establishment of a state income-related scheme in Ireland would therefore dramatically change the environment in which private schemes operate.

Up to recent years, the private pensions sector has been largely autonomous. However, over the past few years there has been increasing concern about the need to monitor and regulate, in an effective manner, the occupational pensions sector. This has partly been because of cases where company pension funds were diverted to help ailing businesses, often leaving the workers without any pension protection if the firm collapsed. Moreover, there are great differences in terms of adequacy of benefit and protection against inflation between the different occupational pension schemes. In general, there has been a need to develop safer methods of funding, to give greater protection to workers in small firms, to provide for the transfer of pension rights in cases where workers change jobs and to give better guarantees of occupational pension indexation in the future. This suggests the need for a greater overseeing or regulatory role by the state.

In October 1985, the then Minister for Social Welfare referred to the growth over the previous twenty years in the coverage of occupational pensions, saying that this led 'to a realisation that government policy and planning in relation to pension provision must embrace both public and private sector activities and must seek a partnership approach to future developments' (Desmond, 1985). He referred to one view of pensions, which was that the social security pensions should remain flat-rate, leaving the occupational pension sector to provide the earnings-related component:

> Would the latter approach create a pension 'elite'? Is there a viable third alternative under which employers would be mandated by legislation to provide occupational pensions for all employees subject to certain qualifying conditions? Is there, indeed, a fourth alternative under which the employer mandate would either be able to provide a company pension scheme or to contribute at a specified level to the personal pension for each employee? What about the supplementary action needed on the government side to regulate the quality and security of occupational pension schemes?

This issue of a national income-related pensions scheme has been current since a discussion paper was published in 1976 (Department of Social Welfare, 1976). The Green Paper showed the gaps that existed in the coverage of state and occupational pension schemes, and specifically that considerable numbers of employees were not covered by an income-related pension scheme. A number of major shortcomings in the coverage of pension schemes were identified: inadequacies in the type and level of pensions, the lack of protection of pension rights on changes of employment, the failure to protect the value of pensions against inflation and the lack of overall coordination in the various provisions for pensions.

Given that the last government document on pensions is the 1976 Green Paper, there is an amount of uncertainty about the likely format of a new state scheme and the role for occupational schemes which would be envisaged. Among the uncertainties, it is not known if the state scheme would permit contracting out, nor whether the scheme would be accompanied by legislation which imposes certain standards on occupational schemes. The latter could be seen as part of a contracting-out option. In addition, since an attraction of private schemes is that they can offer pensions which are a higher proportion of final salary than is the case in the current state scheme, the future demand for private schemes will depend in part on the extent to which pensions in a new state scheme replaced final income. Given the current and prospective constraints on the Irish public finances, it is unlikely that a new state scheme could match the current occupational schemes, especially for those people with relatively high earnings. It is in fact unlikely that any state scheme will emerge in the near future.

The funding of pension provision tends to be associated with private pension provision. However, there could be an element of funding in public social security finance, that is, the setting aside of funds in advance for a liability, such as pension payment, which has to be met. In Canada and in Japan this is done in part.

Disability benefit: The Social Welfare Act of 1952 substituted a single benefit, disability benefit, for the sickness and disablement benefits which were paid under the former national health insurances schemes. In the thirty-year period up to the early 1980s there was a marked rise in the frequency and duration of certified incapacity per person at risk, and in the rate of incapacity. Research results of Hughes (1982) relate to absence from work and the disability benefit scheme. His work uses data on certified incapacity for work. An analysis of the incapacity model indicates that, while alcohol consumption and the weather affect certified incapacity, their influence is weak compared to the effect of the replacement ratio (which measures the extent to which disability benefits replace average earnings when workers become ill), the real wage rate and long-term unemployment. Hughes suggests that the main reason for the increase in the number of claims which has occurred over time is that the pay-related supplement is an additional investment in the health of the labour force which enables workers to take time off work during illness to get the treatment which they need and which they could not afford on flat-rate benefit alone.

Disability benefit is financed by payroll taxes on

employers and employees and by the Exchequer. There have been a number of instances in recent years where suggestions have been made for a reform of the disability benefit system, whereby the employer would pick up some of the responsibility for supporting employees in the initial stages of sickness. One policy option would be whereby employers would be made statutorily responsible for providing such pay during the first weeks of illness: sick pay would then be treated as part of employees' earnings and taxed in the normal way (Hughes, 1982,1988). A number of European countries operate pay schemes along these lines. The data available suggest that the proportion of the insured labour force in Ireland which is covered by occupational sick pay schemes is about 75 per cent of employees. One possibility would be to make the employer responsible for such pay for a specified period in Ireland. In addition to facilitating the taxation of sickness benefit this would

(*a*) eliminate duplication in existing schemes and hence lead to a reduction in public expenditure on sickness benefit;

(*b*) localise the problem within each firm and encourage employers and workers to take responsibility for dealing with it;

(*c*) give employers an incentive to cut down sickness absence rates by, for example, providing better screening procedures and health and safety measures. It might be, however, that appropriate monitoring by the Department of Social Welfare would cut down the need for such a policy change.

In July 1987 the government decided to transfer responsibility for sick pay to employers for an initial period of thirteen weeks. Employers would be compensated in respect of payments for illness made to employees, with detailed arrangements about compensation to be worked out. In fact, this policy change has not been put into effect. The method of compensation which would be used by government in any such policy change would affect crucially the incentives which employers would have to control the level of absenteeism. For instance, the method of compensation used in the U.K. — direct compensation by reducing the social insurance payments made by employers, gaining —led to employers as a group, although not all employers and little or no net gain to government (Disney, 1987).

HEALTH INSURANCE

A major policy debate in Ireland in recent years has concerned the funding of health services, with a government-appointed commission reporting in 1989 on the issue. Ireland has a mixed financial system, midway between the (almost wholly) tax-financed National Health Service system of the UK and the US system which has a large role for private insurance; in Ireland a significant proportion of householders are covered by insurance under Voluntary Health Insurance (VHI) schemes.

From the discussion above on insurance, it is evident that problems about efficiency and equity can arise with private health insurance. The features of private insurance, pointed out above, have implications both for efficiency — already outlined — and for equity. In a world of community rating, which is what the VHI has used up to now, risks are pooled across the risks of different types. As a result those with high risks — including the elderly and those who become chronically ill — are effectively being subsidised by the low-risk groups. In a world of private insurance, the high-risk groups could face prohibitively high premia, or could be denied insurance in the absence of governmental regulation ensuring — as occurs in the case of motor insurance — that nobody can be denied insurance. Moreover, in a world where public and private insurance co-exist, the entry of private insurers would be likely to lead low-risk groups to exit from the public system and enter the system of private finance. In turn, this would leave the public insurance system more unviable than it was before, with consequent increases in premium rates for a group which is on average now a higher risk group than heretofore. The net impact of this would be to increase inequalities, especially when it is borne in mind that there is a correlation between low incomes, unemployment and ill health. Indeed, one of the likely results of a move towards private insurance is that there will be greater demands for policies which will redress the balance for low-income households — whether in the form of government regulation or subsidies (either direct to households or to the VHI). At the very least, there would be need for government monitoring, which would have resource implications. Hence, as in the case of pensions, we find that a policy, which in one dimension may seem to amount to privatisation, may through its consequent and indirect effects work in the opposite direction to privatisation.

In the US, Blue Cross/Blue Shield at first used 'community rating' — somewhat similar to the method adopted by the VHI — whereby all families of a given size paid the same premium. When commercial insurers entered the health insurance market they used 'experience rating', and as a result offered lower premia to low-risk people than the premia available from Blue Cross/Blue Shield. This led Blue Cross/Blue Shield to modify their community rating in order to maintain their market share.

SOME CONCLUSIONS

Some of the main threads can now be drawn together. First, households' well being will depend in part on the combination of market and transfer income which they receive. A greater reliance on private arrangements as a substitute for current social security could lead to greater economic inequality. This is because employer sick pay and pensions (so-called 'occupational welfare') is likely to be distributed across employees in a way which resembles the distribution of market incomes — with regard to elements such as the proportion of earnings which is entitled to be reimbursed, for what period, and conditions such as length of service.

Second, with regard to pension provision, this can be seen as having three dimensions: public pensions, occupational provision and personal retirement savings. There has been an increase in the coverage of occupational pensions, but again there are distinct differences in adequacy of coverage between different people and different types of employment. Related to this is the evidence that there has been an increase in the degree of duality in the labour market: with fissures between those in part-time employment, in temporary or seasonal jobs, in contract employment, in low-paid work with little skill enhancement over time and those in jobs with promotional ladders, on-the-job training and fringe benefits which make up an important part of total remuneration. Those at the bottom end of the labour market are likely to be least well served by occupational benefits. Related to this is whether at some time there should be mandatory occupational pensions.

Third, one cannot look only at one dimension of privatisation. Privatisation in one area, e.g., replacement of private for public provision with regard to pensions or sick pay, can lead to an increase in the role of the state in another area, such as regulation.

Fourth, there is need to take account of public-private interactions. To what extent are people prepared to 'top up' existing public provision by making private arrangements? To what extent should they be encouraged to do so, for example through the tax system? Employers themselves may be prepared to top up only to a defined level of benefit. And those people who are most disadvantaged in the labour market are likely to do little or no topping up. As another example of interaction, if an increase in, say, private pension provision leads to greater inequality in outcomes for reasons given above, there would be a case for a stronger redistributive element in public schemes (e.g., through minimum provisions or through a progressive structure in any earnings-related tier).

Fifth, as indicated above for the UK, some forms of privatisation involve greater risks for individuals. If people make the 'wrong' choices, there are likely to be demands for risk-sharing on the part of the state. This has happened in the US under the Pension Benefits Guarantee Corportation.

Finally, for some people, especially the frail elderly and the disadvantaged, the future issues concern not just privatisation but how to ensure that an appropriate mix of cash transfers and services in kind are delivered. This is a particularly relevant question for the 'very elderly'. Related to this, there is the issue whether there should be an increase in the coverage of social insurance for alternatives to hospital care for the very old: for instance, in nursing homes, sheltered housing, within-home care, day care and respite care. It is likely that some of the high-cost acute-care hospital services for the elderly occur because they are financed by social insurance while alternative (lower cost and more appropriate in cases) forms of care are not so covered.

Thanks are due to Gerard Hughes for comments. The usual disclaimer applies.

TRANSPORT DEREGULATION
AND PRIVATISATION

Sean D. Barrett

Trinity College, Dublin

INLAND TRANSPORT POLICY
Irish inland transport policy has had four phases in the last sixty years:

(*a*) *private sector competition*: this phase ended in the restrictive licensing legislation of 1932 and 1933;

(*b*) *private sector monopoly*: this phase ended with the nationalisation of CIE in 1950;

(*c*) *public sector monopoly*: this phase gradually ended in the late 1970s with liberalisation of road freight on a phased basis and de facto liberalisation of intercity bus services. Road freight was fully deregulated in September 1988;

(*d*) *deregulation and privatisation*: the 1985 Green Paper on Transport Policy, the fare savings from de facto bus deregulation, the spillover impacts of airline deregulation on UK routes, the 1992 internal market, the Irish debt/GNP ratio problem are the factors influencing this phase.

8 *Private sector competition* from about 1925 onwards undoubtedly brought large savings to the users of road transport. At the Annual General Meetings of the Great Southern Railways from 1926 onwards the Chairman complained about the growth of competition. He defended the purchase of the Irish Omnibus Company in 1930 on the grounds that it would 'eliminate wasteful competition'. He complained in 1932 that 'nowhere in the world was the whole matter of road and rail competition allowed to drift as it has been, until quite recently, in Great Britain or the Irish

Free State' (Barrett, 1982, p.3).

The Great Southern Railways was created in 1924 by government intervention to amalgamate twenty-six railways, operating entirely within the Irish Free State. Passenger traffic declined from 15.5 million in 1926 to 11.9 million in 1931. Railway management and shareholders pressed for restraints on competition. This was in the economic spirit of the times. According to Conroy (1928, p.370) 'it would not be inconsistent with the age of "trusts" and "combines" that all competition in the transport world should be eliminated... Road transport should be merely used as a complement for rail transport, not as a substitute for it.'

Private sector monopoly: This was legislated into existence by the Transport Acts of 1932 and 1933. The independent bus and road freight operators were subjected to restrictive licensing and acquisition, either voluntary or compulsory. The effect on the independent bus operators was to cut their passenger numbers from 34.5 million to 1 million (Transport Tribunal, 1939, p.13-14). They were reduced from a position of three times as many passengers as the Great Southern Railways to only a tenth. The number of independent road hauliers was reduced by acquisitions from 1,356 in 1933 to 886 in 1938, (Meenan, p.161). The Pacemaker Report (CIE, 1963, section 111.13) stated that 'it was doubtless intended that all private hauliers would be bought out. The process of buying out stopped, however, and those unacquired thus found themselves in that position more or less by accident.'

The 1939 Transport Tribunal criticised the Great Southern Railway monopoly tradition which the 1932 and 1933 legislation had underpinned. In the Dáil debate on the 1944 Transport Act, which amalgamated the railways and the Dublin bus service, the Minister, Mr Lemass, referred to the failure of the Great Southern Railways to give satisfactory services 'despite the quasi-monopoly which was created for them by legislation' (Dáil Debates, col. 118, vol. 72).

The belief in private sector monopoly in the 1930s was not unique. For example, US internal aviation was organised as a cartel from 1938 to 1978. In Ireland, despite early evidence that the private sector monopoly created in the early 1930s was not efficient, there was no revision of the anti-

8

competitive phase except the transfer of those monopoly powers to the public sector in 1950.

Public sector monopoly: The Minister for Industry and Commerce, Mr Morrisey, gave the following reasons for the nationalisation of public inland transport in 1949 in the Dáil:

> Transport is a vital public service of concern to every individual in the State and intimately affecting every phase of the economic life of the country. We all know that the task of providing a national transport system in this country under modern conditions has proved to be beyond the scope of private enterprise, and also that the compromise between State ownership and private enterprise has not been successful. It is the Government's duty to ensure that such an important service is carried on as effectively and as efficiently as possible. We have come to the conclusion that the discharge of that duty demands State ownership of public transport. (Dáil Debates, col. 55, vol. 110).

Nationalisation was implemented because governments feared bankruptcy in a private sector monopoly created by legislation in the 1930s. There was a belief in the 1930s that a market was prone to bouts of 'wasteful competition'. Having created an unsuccessful private sector monopoly in Irish public transport, the state in 1949-50 was under pressure from both shareholder and labour interests to nationalise public transport. For management the benefits of security in the public sector had obvious advantages over a return to the pre-1932 competitive environment.

Labour governments in Britain also promoted nationalisation. Morrison (1933, p.157) set out the theoretical benefits of nationalisation as better quality of service, lower prices, greater efficiency, and boards which 'must regard themselves as the high custodians of the public interest'. Related goals included a belief that state ownership would confer greater benefits on those with low incomes or in remote regions. In newly independent countries such as Ireland, there was an identification of state enterprises with the national interest. For very large projects only the state would have the borrowing power to finance such projects. Later analysis showed that nationalised transport monopolies increased costs to the economy as a whole and failed to attain the social goals of nationalisation. Bus and train fares were substantially above those in the small independent bus sector (National Prices Commission, 1972). Rather than use CIE services, as intended in legislation, Irish industry bought its own road fleets. In 1964 83 per cent of goods moved in firms' 'own account' vehicles (Central Statistics Office). Ireland cut itself off from the worldwide development of aviation. The doubling of passenger numbers between 1985 and 1988 between Britain and Ireland under deregulation contrasts with decline in the period 1978-85. Since deregulation new airports at Sligo, Knock, Galway, Farranfore and Waterford have opened for international or feeder service. When airport operation was a monopoly no new airport opened in the previous twenty-five years. One of the three state airports was in financial difficulty for virtually all of that period.

The income distribution impacts of transport subsidies could have been tested at any time in this period by use of the Household Budget Survey. Barrett (1982, pp.68-70; 1988) and NESC (1988, p.124) analyse this data and show that 'the top income quintile spent about 10 times as much on transportation as did households in the bottom quintile. The result is a highly regressive State subsidy.'

In regard to remote regions and loss-making routes the state has failed to extract the list of such routes from either a private sector monopoly from 1932 to 1950 or the public sector monopoly since then. Indeed, the Minister has in the Dáil defended CIE's wish not to disclose information (Barrett, 1982, p.22). The National Prices Commission (1973) failed to obtain route costing data to assist it in its work, in spite of stating (Occasional Paper 10, p.45): 'We believe that the practicality of preparing detailed route costings for all services on a continuing basis, or at least, regularly on an ad hoc calculation, should be investigated'

There is no external evidence of board members of state transport companies acting in the public interest, or that they demurred, as Morrison prescribed, from the operation of these monopolies. There is substantial evidence of 'regulatory capture' by the agencies of their government departments (Stigler, 1971). The situation has improved somewhat since the mid-1980s with the growth of staff mobility between government departments, a reassertion of its role by the Department of Finance, a more rigorous approach to public spending and the availability of market alternatives.

The impact of nationalised industry in capital markets has also failed to live up to the goals of the early advocates of nationalisation. Rarely has a dividend been paid to the Exchequer and the debts of public enterprise have been refinanced by 'non-programme outlays' in the Public Capital Programme. Irish capital markets have increased greatly in sophistication since the introduction of the Public Capital Programme in 1950 and can now finance very much larger investments.

We have also evidence that the supply of free or cheap capital to transport undertakings increases capital intensity. Thus CIE proposed the extension of DART to the west of Dublin including an underground section in the centre of Dublin. The National Development Plan 1989-93 opted for the introduction of new diesel commuter services on existing rail lines at a cost of £26 million. This contrasts with £750 million to complete the electrified rail-based system in the Dublin Rail Rapid Transit Study (*Green Paper* 985, p.34). While the period 1980-85 saw intense lobbying by Aer Lingus for funds for fleet replacement, the market has since provided low-cost solutions in the use of non-jet aircraft on low density routes and lower prices to increase load factors and profitability. The capital cost of replacing school buses has also been cut by the possibility of private sector tendering for this service directly rather than through CIE.

The era of deregulation and privatisation: This era has seen the full deregulation of road freight from September 1988 and the de facto deregulation of much of the provincial bus service. From most of the regions of the country there is a daily bus service to Dublin from independents who initially undercut CIE and who have now been joined in competition by Bus Eireann which also undercuts Irish Rail. The passenger is offered the choice between the greater comfort, speed and cost of rail transport and two lower cost alternatives. New services have opened up and frequencies have improved. Airline deregulation on Ireland/UK routes since 1986 is an obvious success. A two-airline cartel has been joined by three new market entrants. Fares have fallen by as much as 65 per cent for those on unrestricted tickets. Business has more than doubled. The regional services have improved out of all proportion as Waterford, Knock, Galway and Kerry enjoy international service without subsidy from public funds. The monopoly of the state companies on policy formulation has been broken.

A number of important developments in economics have stimulated renewed interest in markets and their regulation. Economists such as Elizabeth Bailey, Alfred Kahn and William Baumol were active in the deregulation of US aviation. Their contribution to the economics of regulation was the *theory of contestable markets*. In his presidential address to the American Economics Association (1983) Baumol states that 'the new analysis merely reinforces the view that any proposed regulatory barrier to entry must start off with a heavy presumption against its adoption'.

In a perfectly contestable market, an entrant has access to all production techniques available to incumbents, is not prohibited from wooing the incumbents' customers and entry decisions can be reversed without cost. Efficient allocation of resources is assured by the ease of potential entry, even though the number of firms may be small. Potential entrants are sufficient to ensure that no firm can earn monopoly profits in the long run, that the industry will always be composed of the number of firms that can produce its output at minimum cost, and that in the long run the price of the product must equal its marginal cost.

A further important contribution to our understanding of markets is the work of Demsetz. When competition *in* a market is not possible, Demsetz (1968) recommends competition *for* a market. In natural monopolies such as air traffic control, it has been found that competitive tendering has reduced costs. Market competition was not possible, and without competitive tendering economic rent was earned by the producers.

The third strand in the work of economists in rediscovering markets is that of the social choice school. Buchanan, Downs, Niskanen, Tullock and others have pointed out the returns to individuals and organisations from lobbying governments. Proposals can succeed where the costs are imposed on a large number of people in relatively small amounts while the benefits are lower than costs but concentrated on a small number of people. The power of producers and lobbyists undermines the naive view that governments merely reflect voter preferences.

The fourth strand in favouring new interest among economists in deregulation and privatisation has been the work of the Brookings Institution and the Institute of Economic Affairs on bankruptcy. Bankruptcy, receiverships and liquidations are the operation of market forces in the critical role of transferring assets away from failed managements to those who might use those assets more efficiently. The assets themselves are not destroyed but simply transferred to better managements, if not on the first transfer, then, on a subsequent one. The recent abolition of Foir Teoranta represents acceptance of this view in the industrial sector (Schultze, 1983; Burton, 1983).

Thus there is a wider range of policy options than ever available in choosing transport policy instruments in the 1990s. These options are based on the success of deregulation policies in Ireland and elsewhere, the insights of the theory of contestable markets and competition *for* markets, and new perspectives on bankruptcy which has heretofore mesmerised policy making in transport.

THE ECONOMIC CASE FOR GOVERNMENT INTERVENTION REVISITED

The economic case for government intervention is based on market failure in a sector. For example, the lack of a pricing system for urban road use presents difficulties for buses. They are an efficient user of scarce urban road space and would therefore fare well in a market with road pricing. A second best solution is government intervention to support the bus services by subsidy. The second best solution runs the risk, however, that the subsidy may be absorbed in inefficiency or a transfer to either the employees or managers of the subsidised company. In the case of a private company the benefit of the subsidy might accrue to the shareholders. If road pricing is ruled out by policy makers exclusive bus lanes might be used as an intervention in favour of the bus because of its greater efficiency in the use of urban road space.

Externalities in a market may lead to too much of an item being produced when there are external diseconomies and too little when there are external economies. Thus the case for government intervention to assist railways is made on the basis that a growth of road transport as a result of the withdrawal of rail services would leave society as a whole worse off. This is also second best solution when compared with a direct restriction of the externalities arising from road transport, for example, measures to reduce road traffic accidents. Where railways are subsidised because road users do not meet their infrastructure costs the first best solution is to derive an appropriate tax structure for heavy goods vehicles. When rail passengers enjoy significant time savings which would be lost by transfer to road these could be incorporated in the railway revenues by appropriate pricing of express trains compared to slow trains.

At present, government intervention in the competition between road and rail transport is designed to restrict the output of the road sector for reward and to fund the deficits of railways. To equate the deficit of the railways with any measure of social benefits from railways without analysis is unlikely to equilibrate social cost and benefits.

Bayliss (1981, p.164) describes the state of railways subsidisation as follows:

> The Federal Republic of Germany is not alone in assisting the railways at enormous cost to the nation, with little attempt to consider whether policy objectives could be met more effectively by other means. It is essential that rail subsidies policy be based upon strict economic and policy arguments, and that the cost effectiveness of such policies in relation to other instruments and policies be accurately assessed.

MARKET INVESTMENT IN TRANSPORT

Will the market, left to itself, seriously underinvest in transport? The historical evidence is that this was not the case. Kelsey (1986) stated that in 1885 there were 467 transport companies quoted on the London Stock Exchange with a nominal value of £750 million. The transport sector represented 14 per cent of all companies quoted (Chartered Institute of Transport, 1986). The 1985 value of transport companies on the London Stock Exchange was about £250 billion. The value of the transport companies actually quoted in 1985 was only £2.8 billion. In 1885 transport accounted for 14 per cent of all companies quoted. In 1985 it accounted for only 1.3 per cent. Government policies of nationalisation, and not market forces, wiped out investors' interest in the transport sector. In 1982, according to Peter Lazarus (1984), 'the total use of resources in transport in the UK amounted to some £50 billion, of which only about £5 billion was public expenditure'. While investment in transport companies has declined in relative terms, the bulk of transport investment as a whole is carried out by the private sector.

SECTORAL ANALYSIS OF TRANSPORT PRIVATISATION AND DEREGULATION

In this section the transport industry is examined by sector, and the implications of deregulation and privatisation are examined and lessons drawn from experience in Britain.

Road freight: This sector was restricted as part of the policy of creating a private sector monopoly in 1933. The number of operators was reduced through acquisition by railway companies from 1,356 to 886 between 1933 and 1938. Through the Act it was hoped 'to make it possible for the Great Southern Railway in its area and other railway companies in their areas to establish themselves in what is described as a monopoly position'. The process of buying-out stopped, however, and those unacquired thus found themselves in that position more or less by accident (Barrett, 1982, p.13). In 1938 the Chairman of the Great Southern Railways complained of 'widespread and ingenious evasion' of the 1933 Act and of the number of hauliers still operating. The Transport Tribunal of 1939 recommended the acquisition of the remaining road hauliers with state compensation equal to the aggregate of four years' profits.

The position changed little following nationalisation. In a submission to the Beddy Committee in 1956, CIE proposed that 'all commercial vehicles would be limited in their area of operation. Initially this limit was proposed at fifty miles for one year. The limit would be reduced each year until the full capacity of the railways is achieved.' This proposal was not accepted but the protectionist policies of the time were exemplified in the Transport Act, 1956, which decreed that vehicle leasing was the equivalent of licensed haulage for hire or reward and was therefore subject to quantity licensing.

In 1964 the CSO found that the market shares of Irish road haulage were 83 per cent own account, 11 per cent licensed haulage and 6 per cent CIE road haulage. Very gradual liberalisation commenced with the deregulation of the carriage of cattle, sheep and pigs in 1970 and the removal of weight, area and commodity restrictions on licensed hauliers. Total liberalisation was envisaged in the 1976 Road Transport Bill but did not occur until September 1988 because of the opposition of the licence holders. Expansion in haulage under the 1978 Road Transport Act was confined to licence holders.

The faults of road haulage licensing were the excessive traffic movements on 'own account', the economic rent enjoyed by licence holders due to entry restrictions, the bans on backloading and vehicle leasing. The cost to Irish industry was estimated at some 11 per cent of total freight costs in 1980. The value of a road haulage licence was estimated at £5,000 in 1973 by the National Prices Commission. This is the equivalent of £29,000 at 1990 prices.

Table 1 shows the productivity changes and market changes in the sector since 1980. The market share of licensed haulage doubled to 89 per cent of total receipts. Its productivity was on average 120 per cent greater than that of CIE, according to the unweighted average of the six productivity indices in the table.

Privatisation of road freight. CIE's share of the total goods vehicle fleet is even lower when one takes account of the own account sector. There are approximately 100,000 goods vehicles registered in the 1986 vehicle census, of which 340 are in the CIE fleet.

In Britain the privatisation of the National Freight Consortium in 1982 has been an undoubted success story. Eighty-three per cent of the company was bought by employees, the firm's pensioners and their families. Seventeen per cent was held by the banks who provided the

Table 1

Licensed Hauliers and Railway Company Shares of Road Freight, 1970-86

	Miles run (million)		Tons carried (million)		Vehicles		Staff		Receipts (£m)	
	L	R	L	R	L	R	L	R	L	R
1970	30.1	18.3	5.7	3.8	1,051	1,101	1,851	2,999	4.5	5.7
1980	89.6	11.5	12.7	2.2	2,386	673	3,778	1,334	63.8	13.6
1986	123.5	7.1	17.5	1.2	2,816	340	4,098	852	120.5	14.9

L = licensed haulier   R = railway company

Productivity Indices of CIE and Licensed Hauliers, 1986

	CIE	Licensed Haulage	Index (CIE = 100)
Miles run per vehicle	20,882	43,856	210
Tons carried per vehicle	3,529	6,214	176
Vehicle miles per staff	8,333	30,137	362
Tons carried per staff	1,408	4,270	303
Receipts per vehicle (£)	43,824	42,791	98
Receipts per staff (£)	17,488	29,405	168

Licensed Hauliers Market Shares (%)

	1970	1986
Miles run	62	95
Tonnage carried	60	94
Vehicle numbers	49	89
Staff employed	38	83
Receipts	44	89

Source: Irish Statistical Bulletin September 1988.

finance for the purchase of the company. The company lost £4.37 million in 1981. Its profits in 1982 were £10.1 million, in 1985 £27.2 million and in 1988, £90 million. In March 1989 the institutions raised their share to 20 per cent. The current market capitalisation of the firm is £854 million. Vickers and Yarrow (p.164) state that 'the fact that National Freight has become such a thriving business underlines the importance of good incentives structures — achieved in this case by the employee buy-out — in determining the success of privatisation'.

The bus industry: The anti-competitive phase of bus industry regulation began with the Road Transport Act, 1932, which prohibited the operation of scheduled passenger services for individual stage-carriage transport. In the Dáil the Minister for Industry and Commerce, Mr McGilligan, stated that while the tendency in the Act was

> to divert traffic into the hands of the three transport companies operating on a big scale at present ... we do allow for the existence side by side with these three agencies of the independent bus proprietor or company. Personally, I look forward to seeing these people disappearing by degrees either by the process of amalgamation with other companies or by the main companies deciding that their future lay in certain areas in the country and leaving other areas for exploitation by independent bus owners (Dáil Debates, vol. 40, para. 26327).

In 1933 his successor, Mr Lemass, was more explicit in limiting the role of the independent transport company. In his restriction of competition in road freight in the 1933 Road Transport Act he hoped 'to make it possible for the Great Southern Railway in its area and the other railway companies in their areas to establish themselves in what is described as a monopoly position' (Senate Debates, vol. 16, para. 979)

Table 2 shows the pattern of acquisition of independent bus service licences by the statutory companies over the years 1933-41. One thousand and ninety-eight bus service licences were acquired, 99 per cent of them by the three major companies.

The market for bus services: In the late 1960s the independent bus sector showed signs of revival. The National

Table 2

Transfers of Independent Bus Service Licences to Statutory Transport Companies, 1933-41

	1933	1934	1935	1936	1937	1938	1940	1941	
to Great Southern Railways									
voluntary	459*	157	11	1	2	2	1	1	
compulsory	1	55	191	9	17	–	–	2	
Great Northern Railways									
voluntary	5	1	4	–	1	1	–	–	
compulsory	12	1	78	–	–	–	–	–	
Dublin United Tramways									
voluntary	–	18	–	–	–	–	–	–	
compulsory	–	47	–	5	–	–	–	–	
Total									
voluntary	464	176	15	1	3	3	1	1	664
compulsory	13	103	269	14	17	–	–	2	418

Notes: There were no transfers in 1939. Transfers to remaining railway companies were 10 in 1934, 3 in 1935, and 3 in 1938.
*446 licences held by a subsidiary company up to 31 December 1933

Source: Barrett (1982).

Prices Commission (1972, p.27) found that the thirty-seven licensed provincial bus operators 'most of them small and many of them operating remote rural routes ... generally charge lower fares and in some cases much lower, than CIE'.

In 1982 the CIE Expressway provincial bus fare was 82 per cent higher than that charged by the Midland Bus Company on the Athlone-Mullingar route and 69 per cent greater than the average of Midland, Shamrock (Clonmel-Thurles), Wharton (Cavan-Longford) and Kavanagh (Urlingford-Kilkenny).

Barrett (1982) estimated that the return coach fare Dublin-Cork would be between £5.40 and £4.80 compared to the excursion rail fare of £13.50. The normal rail fare was £27.00.

On most routes to Dublin the de facto deregulation of bus services has provoked a competitive response from Bus Eireann, even where this involved competition with Irish Rail. The pattern of this competition is normally that CIE, road and rail, decides to 'take on' an independent operator by selectively cutting fares and increasing frequency. For example, in July 1988 Bus Eireann followed private operators Cronin and O'Mahony on to the Cork and Tralee routes to Dublin. CIE has the advantages of national marketing and identified city bus depots in meeting this competition. On the other hand, there is little evidence of economies of scale in bus operation, and local operators may be better placed to meet local market needs.

In many other respects, however, there is no level playing field in public policy towards the independent bus service in Ireland.

— CIE has an annual subsidy of £110m in 1989. It is not obvious that Bus Eireann is a stand-alone company which is independent of this subsidy. The Bus Eireann subsidy is £3.4 million.

— CIE borrowings are part of the Public Sector Borrowing Requirement. This reduces the cost of funds by two percentage points and increases the supply. By contrast, many independent bus companies use hire purchase.

— CIE receives first option on the school transport contract, worth £26.2 million in 1989. CIE then decides how much it wishes to subcontract to the private sector — a reversal of the case normally made *for* nationalisation.

— Where CIE's competitors seek an extension to a route or a new route for individual stage carriage these proposals are sent to CIE rather than assessed by an independent authority. There is no right of appeal against the decisions and CIE has the benefit of its competitors' market research.

— Only the minority of CIE's competitors who have stage-carriage licences are permitted to carry those in the free travel scheme for old people. CIE gives the Department a discount of 40 per cent on these passengers. Most of the independent bus services offer larger discounts but are not permitted to serve this market which in 1988 cost £27.2 million.

Deregulation of bus services: The 1985 Green Paper on Transport Policy sets out the arguments for and against bus deregulation as shown in Table 3. The case against deregulation is that it involves a reduction in safety, loss of an integrated network, loss of service on thin routes, loss of cross-subsidisation, and loss of demand for CIE services. On the other hand, safety of vehicles is a matter for the PSV (Public Service Vehicle) Office of the Gardai and the abolition of this office has not been proposed. The passenger will decide whether the bus service should run as a single entity rather than on a point-to-point basis. There is no evidence of substantial passenger transfers between routes at present. Many of the licensed private operators and Irish hire services operated in remote areas because neither CIE nor the Great Southern Railways wanted to serve such areas. These include Cavan, Monaghan, Donegal, North Kerry and West Cork from which the railways withdrew. Cross-subsidisation means the charging of some passengers above long-run marginal cost and others below. It runs the risk that passengers so being overcharged will cease to pay this form of taxation. Lower cost producers will be able to serve more remote areas without cross-subsidisation. What happens to CIE's traffic in a deregulated market depends on how the company reacts to the new environment.

In relation to the public service forms of transport, such as carriage of the old and school transport, markets worth £54 million in 1988-9, there should be Demsetz tendering to get

Table 3

Arguments for and against Liberalisation of Bus Services

FOR

Customers would benefit from competition in terms of fare levels and quality of service.

Market supply would adjust to passenger demand, thereby producing more effective and economical use of transport resources.

Would challenge CIE and its staff, giving them an opportunity to respond to competition in the market place.

A licensing system would provide a means for controlling the very considerable transport operations which are at present legally doubtful.

Would encourage experimentations with minibuses and small buses particularly as replacements on routes where the use of large buses is uneconomic due to low levels of demand.

Success of private operators would help to convince CIE to withdraw from certain areas (or services) thereby leading to improved CIE financial performance; also increased competition might help the railways to be more cost effective.

AGAINST

Risk that unrestricted competition would adversely affect the quality of service, with safety implications.

Full liberalisation might lead to gaps in services rather than in integrated network.

Operators would concentrate routes with high demand leaving CIE to service the low demand routes.

Benefit of cross-subsidisation within CIE would be eroded, as CIE reduced fares on well-supported routes in order to retain traffic.

Possibility of reduction in CIE staff on foot of a fall in demand for CIE services, with redundancy and other cost implications.

Competition would reduce CIE's share of bus traffic in the short-term at least, and possibly cause a further fall in rail passenger traffic levels. This would adversely affect CIE's financial position and could lead to the Board having to reduce its costs (by eliminating and/or reducing uneconomic services).

Source: Green Paper on Transport Policy, 1985, p.23.

the best deal for the Exchequer. The UK experience (Kilvington, 1985) is that competition *for* the bus market has been more successful than competition *in* the market. Nonetheless the deregulation of intercity coaches in 1980 reduced fares and journey times and improved services. The National Bus Company performed better than the new market entrants because of its control of city coach stations, marketing advantages, and, perhaps, some below-cost selling. 'The policy adopted by National Express bears some signs of a campaign of predatory pricing, but, whether or not this is so, the competition authorities stood by and did nothing.' (Vickers and Yarrow, p.374).

Privatisation of UK bus services: The form of privatisation adopted was management buy-out. The company is being sold as fifty-two separate local bus companies, six coach-operating companies, and eight engineering companies. National Express, National Holidays, National Travelworld and the Coach Station subsidiary are also to be privatised (Vickers and Yarrow, p.282). Management buy-outs were favoured by the provision of £50,000 for legal expenses and by allowing such bids to fall up to 5 per cent below outside offers. The anticipated revenue from the privatisation of the National Bus Company is £306 million. This could have been increased by privatisation of the company as a single entity. The economic rents from this degree of protection would have been reflected in the sale price, but competition with the privatised monolith would have been virtually impossible. The competitive privatisation of the National Bus Company was, in part, a response to sustained criticism of the unitary privatisation of the British Airports Authority.

Airports: The British Airports Authority was privatised in August 1987 as a single entity encompassing the London airports of Heathrow, Gatwick and Stansted; the Scottish lowlands airports of Glasgow, Prestwick and Edinburgh; and Aberdeen. These airports handle 73 per cent of UK air passengers and 85 per cent of the cargo tonnage. About half the BAA's income comes from charges to airlines and half from concessionaires who sell goods, including duty-free, at the airport shops. Twenty per cent of the BAA's income comes from the sale of duty-free. This subsidy to airports and airlines from taxpayers in general is due to be abolished for travel within the EC after 1992. The profit of BAA was £54 million in 1981, £82 million in 1985 and £124 million in 1987. The 1988 profit was £166 million and the estimate for 1989 is £220 million. The market capitalisation of the company is £1,885 million. The issue price in 1987 was £500 million. The market capitalisation of BAA includes substantial economic rents from the above items, plus ground handling monopolies, the allocation of landing rights by the 'grandfather rights' system and control over 94 per cent of passenger traffic in the London area.

The case for privatising BAA as a single entity and against competing airports was made by Bayfield (1984) and Foster (1984). Bayfield states that 'the practical difficulties of gaining official approval to build a new airport, and the long lead time before the substantial capital investment required begins to show returns, virtually rule out the competitive threat which would be posed by new entrants'. Foster recommends single entity sale of the BAA because 'it would provide the benefits of careful planning in a reasonably well-defined environment, as well as the lower costs that come from efficient use of economies of scale and particularly of joint production. This in turn means that the Authority would be able to raise funds more cheaply and its sale price would better reflect its true value.' According to Foster (1984), competition between airports 'is likely to prove largely illusory' for the following reasons:

(*a*) the product is diverse, varying by time as well as by place. Different consumers want different attributes not readily provided at each of these airports;

(*b*) it is difficult for airports to compete on price, since airport charges are only a small proportion of airline costs — rarely more than five per cent;

(*c*) only a small number of airports can be viable, given economies of scale in operation;

(*d*) revenue from privatising airports separately may well be less than if the Authority is sold as a single entity because of greater uncertainty as well as more limited market power, and uncertainty about how the new airport system would operate;

(*e*) the long-run planning of an airport system almost

inherently requires an overall strategy for investment or entails the risk of underinvestment.

All of these points can be disputed. *Product diversity* is not an argument against competition. Consumers trade off between products which are not identical. In transport this typically occurs in the trade-off between speed, quality of service and price. *Airports and related charges* account for 25.9 per cent of the cost of airline journey in Europe. Lack of competition at and between airports leads to increased fares (EEC, 1984). *Economies of scale* are not obvious in comparing airports of different sizes in Britain. For example, Gatwick has only a tenth of Manchester's profits with twice as many passengers. Edinburgh in 1982-3 lost £1.3 million on the same number of passengers as East Midlands which had a profit of £1.1 million. Gloucester-Cheltenham made profits on an income which was one-fourteenth of Stansted, which lost £4.6 million. *Investment planning* — long lead times and high costs are not inevitable. The London City Airport cost £7 million and had a forty-week construction period. *The sale price* reflects economic rents such as BAA's virtual monopoly in the London area. There has been underinvestment at Heathrow and Gatwick and substantial cross-subsidisation of Stansted and Prestwick. In the event, the BAA management secured the type of privatisation they sought with an RPI-X formula for price control. Competitive airport privatisation, on the other hand, would have allowed airlines, the customers of the airports, to trade one off against the other, as passengers do now in deregulated airline markets. With competing airports pricing would be something more than mere cost recovery.

Competition between airports would force airport managements to examine their costs and the many anti-competitive practices at airports. The latter have been criticised by the Monopolies and Mergers Commission (1983, 1985). They include allocation of airport slots by 'grandfather rights' to older airlines, bans on new market entrants, bans on competition in ground handling and lack of competition in air traffic control.

Competitive privatisation of airports includes Demsetz tendering for air traffic control both at airports and for national airspace (Barrett, 1987). Such tenders have been successfully implemented at Liverpool, Exeter, Perth and Bournemouth. At the latter airport, IAL operated with twenty-six staff, compared to the Civil Aviation Authority's forty-two. Having lost out in the earlier tendering the CAA won Manchester in 1985 after a full review of its costs when faced with a competitive tender (1985, p.1).

Airports exhibit no public-good characteristics of importance. Public control has restricted investment in many parts of Europe in both airport capacity and ATC services. Given the growth in air transport, and that air passengers pay for these services in their ticket prices, airports and ATC are attractive investment opportunities (Barrett, 1984, 1989).

In Ireland Aer Rianta should be privatised as competing airports. Ground handling monopolies should be abolished before privatisation. ATC should be constituted as a separate plc and then privatised and exposed to competitive tendering. Most of the cost of Galway and Kerry Airports has been subscribed privately. In addition, Knock and Waterford are viable on a day-to-day basis. Aer Rianta is now a highly profitable company and has increased its profitability by 50 per cent since the 1986 deregulation on UK routes. The other Irish regional airports have lower costs and will have handled over 350,000 passengers in 1989.

Airlines: In the immediate post-war period European aviation was organised as a cartel with price coordination, capacity provided in advance and bans on new entrants. The system was an economic burden for an outer offshore island. It gave Europe the dearest air fares in the world according to the annual ICAO fare surveys, and fares about three times those charged by Europe's independent airlines, who operated in a more liberal regulatory system for charter flights to sun destinations. The share of the latter has increased to almost half of the passenger miles flown within geographical Europe. The Ireland/UK deregulation has become a classic illustration of the high costs of allowing a cartel to determine policy. It also illustrates the consequences for users of regulatory capture.

The Anglo-Irish air cartel undersupplied the market which declined from 1.95 million to 1.85 million from 1978 to 1985. The market was opened to competition in May 1986. Passenger number increased to 2.7 million in 1987, 3.6

million in 1988 and an estimated 4.2 million in 1989. This is 2.3 times the cartel level of traffic. The CAA (1987) found that the price of a London-Dublin air fare increased by 75 per cent above the UK inflation rate between 1980 and 1985. Under competition it has fallen by as much as two-thirds. The cartel restricted the supply of discounted fares, in particular at peak times, by use of computer yield management programmes. The largest increase in travel under competition has occurred at the peak months. Since Aer Lingus was only a marginally profitable airline when charging high fares, we must conclude that a large part of the economic rent from protectionism was wasted in inefficiency. Some may have gone in above-market wages, and this is confirmed by the introduction of a two-tier wage structure since deregulation.

Three barriers to competition in European aviation were abolished on Ireland/UK routes in 1986. These were

— the ban on new entrants
— the ban on price competition
— the ban on capacity competition

Under deregulation the passenger is obviously better off, and Aer Lingus has increased its profits. While the airline reduced employment by 1,000 between 1980 and 1985, it has increased employment by 500 since then. The old nationalised industry argument that there would be cross-subsidisation of thin routes from busy ones is proved wrong on both counts by deregulation. Fares are now lower than under the cartel and on new routes such as Knock, Waterford, Galway and Kerry which the cartel did not serve.

Barriers to airline contestability: US research on deregulation by Bailey (1988) and Kahn (1988) shows that established airlines have erected new barriers to contestability as follows:

— control of hub airports
— control of ground handling
— control of computer reservations systems
— geographical price discrimination
— anticompetitive mergers

To these we should add regulatory capture at both national and EC level by the European state airlines. The next stage of promoting the contestability of European aviation is to tackle the above obstacles with policy measures such as the following:

— neutral allocation of slots between new and incumbent carriers at hub airports such as Heathrow, Frankfurt, Paris, Dusseldorf, Rome, Milan etc. This could be done by either auction or lottery.

— The end of ground handling monopolies. Despite the airline deregulation between Ireland and the UK the ground handling monopolies have not been tackled. British Midland estimates that it could halve its Heathrow ground handling costs were it allowed to handle for itself rather than face a choice between British Airways, its major competitor, or another airline with 'grandfather rights' to handle at Heathrow.

— Computer reservation systems are used to bias travel agents' displays against small airlines. If neutrality is not possible then airlines with ownership of CRS system should be forced to divest themselves of this source of bias (Levine, 1987).

— Geographical price discrimination was widely practised in the US by the large airlines. Frequently higher cost incumbent airlines use predatory pricing to put lower cost new entrants out of business.

— Anticompetitive mergers: the merger between BA and British Caledonian at a price over three times the value of the assets was obviously a bid for slots and licences. While the EC managed to dilute the anticompetitive aspects of the merger it did allow the removal from the market of a major potential competitor in a deregulated European aviation scene. Other proposed mergers include Air France and Aer Inter and Sabena with KLM and British Airways.

— All but one of the EC Transport Ministers owns an airline. Aviation is thus treated far more leniently than other cartels by the EC. The Luxembourg package of December 1987 made minimal provision for market entry, no reduction in the unrestricted fares charged by Europe's national carriers and no provision to improve the Commission's ineffectual regional air services directive. Under Article 85.3 of the Rome Treaty, intended to promote economic development and the consumer interest, the airlines were exempted from the competition policy provision in respect of fare collusion, ground handing, CRS, and airport slot allocation.

The European Court has ruled against European air transport policy both in 1986 under the Nouvelles Frontière case and in 1989 in the Ahmed Saeed case.

The privatisation of Europe's airlines might improve contestability in two ways. Under private ownership the high air fares charged in Europe would be reflected in supernormal profits. These are likely to attract more attention than economic rents dissipated in inefficiency or labour costs, as occurs in nationalised industries. The second gain is that privatisation would end the monopoly of regulatory capture by Europe's airlines over their 'parent' government departments. Ministers would no longer be caught in the dilemma of owning an airline and regulating the market with fairness to airlines which they do not own.

British Airways was privatised in 1987 with its monopolistic entitlements attached. It had made losses of £108 million as recently as 1982. Its 1986 profit was £195 million and this increased to £228 millon in 1988 and a projected £225 million in 1989. The current market capitalisation is £1,412 million and the sale price was £985 million. The privatisation of British Airways with its monopolistic properties attached might, at least in theory, allow the government to adopt a more liberal policy in line with overall economic efficiency criteria. On the other hand, shareholders might react against changing the rules to abolish or curtail economic rents after privatisation.

On routes where anti-competitive aviation policies are pursued, such as Germany and Italy, supernormal revenues could be used to cross-subsidise competition on liberalised routes, such as Ireland-UK. It is not possible for the liberal country to reduce fares without the agreement of the anti-competitive country. However, the economic rent could be reduced by selling route licences separately from the airline. This type of auction would have identified the economic rent. The bids would have reflected the efficiency gains of the least cost operator and the revenues would have accrued to the government rather than the airline. The Civil Aviation Authority (1984, p.16) rejected the selling of route licences because 'route licences are not property. British Airways did not purchase its licences and the licence fees and charges which it, like other airlines, has paid in respect of such licences over the years do not in any way reflect the profit expectation arising from their use.'

The CAA criticism here ignores economic reality. While access to European air routes remains restricted, incumbent airlines enjoy a property right. The value of the property right can be ascertained by selling the licences separately from the physical assets of the airline.

Shipping/Ports: Sealink was sold to the Sea Containers Group in 1984 for £66 million. Irish Ferries was rescued from the collapse of Irish Shipping and operates as a commercial company. In acquisition costs, losses and equity injections the B & I Line has already cost three times as much as Sealink, and the possibility of a sale on the Stock Exchange or to Irish Ferries should be considered. The 1985 Green Paper (p.62) is unconvincing in its reasons for the Irish government's acquisition of the B & I Line. There is no doubt that the existence of an Irish-controlled company has avoided the possible abuse of a dominant position where monopoly power could be exerted or service interrupted. For a part of the period the B & I Line operated a cartel with Sealink. Much freight traffic used the Larne routes where competition operated without government intervention. The availability of government finance appears to have exacerbated the Line's financial problems. In the period 1979 to 1984 the B & I Line's annual financial charges grew by an estimated 41 per cent and labour costs per employee by 16 per cent in real terms. Associated British Ports was formerly the British Transport Docks Board. It was privatised for £70 million in 1981 and 1984. Two and a half per cent of the stock is held by the employees. It has nineteen facilities in Britain, including Southampton, Hull and Cardiff. The market capitalisation of the company is currently £523 million. The share price was 56p in 1983 and in mid-1989 stood at 596p.

The success of ABP has been in its diversification into property and operation of facilities on behalf of the shipping companies. The Report of the Dublin Docks Review Group (Chairman John Horgan) points to the cumbersome Board structure of the major Irish port. 'A Board of 23 members, none of whom is paid and many of whom will naturally see themselves as representatives of special interests, could hardly be expected to provide the strong, competent and united leadership which the development of Dublin Port requires' (p.37). Privatisation should also be considered for Dublin and all port authorities such as Dun Laoghaire and Rosslare, as well as those operated under the Harbours Acts by quasi-local authorities.

Railways: The entire cycle of unprofitable state involvement in transport began with the attempts to rescue the railways almost sixty years ago. Is privatisation of the railways possible? How much would it save?

It is likely that railways would have to be privatised with their subsidies intact. Barrett (1982) estimates that in 1979 about half the subsidy to Irish railways was absorbed in employing labour surplus to manning at British Railways levels of productivity. Competitive tendering would, over time, erode the wasteful consequences of subsidy and in some cases, perhaps, erode it completely.

Currently some 40 per cent of freight wagons on British Rail are privately owned. When coal traffic is excluded the proportion rises to over 85 per cent (Gotch, 1987). The Orient Express is an example of a privately-owned train in the passenger market.

Starkie (1986) proposed the privatisation of British Rail trains to competing operators with competitive bidding for slots within the system which is probably still a natural monopoly. Railways in the US are privately owned, and the Japanese Railways were privatised in 1988. In Britain there might also be scope to privatise separately the main businesses of the railways and to restore the former regions which were amalgamated to form British Rail.

PRIVATISATION BENEFITS
The economic benefits of privatisation include the substitution of ownership of real assets, shares, for non-negotiable assets such as the citizen's shareholding in a nationalised enterprise. The new ownership can improve the role of labour and management as the experiences of the National Freight Consortium and the National Bus Company

indicate. The position of the citizen is improved by the market in privatised company stock.

Privatisation creates a market in corporate control. The threat of bankruptcy is a major incentive which is lost by nationalisation. The market gives an independent evaluation of management performance. By contrast, government departments, parliamentary committees and the conscripted shareholders of public enterprises are powerless to assess efficiency in the face of regulatory capture.

In Ireland, which has a large public debt, the gains from debt reduction, even on a once-off basis, are better than no debt reduction. Once-off debt reduction would allow tax reductions which would improve work incentives and permit a reduction of the extremely high taxation of labour.

Much of the rationale for public involvement in transport in Ireland and elsewhere was without economic rationale. In the anticompetitive policies towards truck, bus and airline competition, government intervention has imposed substantial costs on a small open economy.

Government intervention in transport has usually resulted in increased costs, and deregulation will therefore continue to bring reduced costs. Privatisation is an essential adjunct to deregulation given the difficulties posed by regulatory capture and the requirement that Ministers deal impartially where they own a company in a business they regulate.

Since transport is basically a market function the privatisation of transport is not likely to present any difficulties in the economy as a whole. It would allow the public sector to refocus on its pure public goods functions while leaving the market to do what it does best.

PRIVATISATION IN THE COMMUNICATIONS INDUSTRY

John Bristow

Trinity College, Dublin

This paper deals with telecommunications only and ignores posts. Of course, the distinction between them is becoming increasingly blurred by technical advances, but it should be clear that what is meant by posts is the traditional letter and parcel service. This is left out of the reckoning because I know of no country where there is not a publicly owned service of this kind. So there is no evidence about the privatisation of posts, which is methodologically of some importance to me.

Public discussion of privatisation — and, regrettably, many allegedly 'scientific' pronouncements from within the economics profession on this subject — consist excessively of prescriptions based solely on *a priori* reasoning. Mystical incantantions such as 'contestability' and 'principal-agent relations' are recited as sole support for assertions that, respectively, society does not need to break up or regulate monopolies and that it makes a difference to efficiency whether a firm is publicly or privately owned. In fact, contestability theory is extremely sensitive to the truth of some pretty implausible assumptions and the evidence on the relative efficiency of public and private enterprise becomes more ambiguous as it accumulates.

Would any sane person take a drug because biochemical theory says it cures a disease? Would such a person not want pretty thorough empirical testing of the drug first? I make no apology for requiring the same kind of empiricism when it comes to major social medication such as privatisation. We have some evidence about the privatisation of telecommunications within the same kind of governmental and administrative tradition as we have in this country, and most of this paper will be devoted to the lessons to be learned from that evidence. I refer of course to British Telecommunications plc.

Unfortunately, it is my view that the BT experience does not tell us a great deal about whether privatisation improves efficiency, because practically everything which the British government has done in relation to the privatisation of telecommunications suggests that improved efficiency has not been one of its objectives. Still, we have something to go on.

I want to concentrate on market structure rather than ownership because there is both firmer theoretical support and stronger evidence for the importance to efficiency of the former than the latter. So, let us remind ourselves of the main features of telecommunications which are relevant to the emergence or maintenance of one market structure rather than another. Four features strike me as being particularly important:

(*a*) the existence of economies of scale in the traditional product which are very pronounced in local networks and may remain unexhausted in the average European national network;

(*b*) rapid technical progress, both in the way the old things are done (voice communication) and in the invention of new products (machine-readable data transmission and storage, etc.);

(*c*) significant, continuous upward shifts in demand functions. In the domestic market, telephones have a high income-elasticity of demand. In the business sector, the demand shift is related to the change in industrial structure towards more communications-intensive activities;

(*d*) the existence of multiple products which, as intermediate goods, possess high marginal rates of technical substitution.

The first and third of these give great opportunities for monopolistic exploitation. The second and fourth give opportunities for entry by new producers although, if the existing, dominant producer can use the legal environment to keep out new entrants, those features also create increased opportunities to earn monopoly rents.

(Economists will appreciate some rather juicy externality issues in this industry. First, the connection of a new consumer imposes congestion costs on existing consumers but also gives existing consumers a benefit because there is an extra person they can contact by telephone. Secondly, traditionally the call charge is billed to the caller, whereas both parties benefit from the call. These things are central to the design of optimal tariffs, but will be pursued no further here.)

We now turn to BT. Until 1969, this was part of the Post Office — a department of government. In that year it was turned into a public corporation, though still having the sixty-year-old legal monopoly of the traditional business. That went in 1981 and, in 1984, BT was 50.2 per cent privatised. It was of course not the first British privatisation, but it was the biggest to date and, more significantly for us, the first involving a major public utility.

I shall not be discussing the flotation of the BT stock, except to say that it revealed a great deal about the British government's privatisation objectives. Dominating all else were two factors. First, fear that the issue would be undersubscribed, thus making life very difficult when it came to implementing the intended, subsequent privatisations. Secondly, a desire to use this flotation as an instrument towards the objective of more widespread stock ownership (only 7 per cent of British adults owned corporate stock, compared with 25 per cent in the US). These factors explain what by normal standards could hardly be claimed as a masterpiece of corporate finance. More interestingly, it showed that revenue-maximisation was nowhere near the top of the government's list of objectives.

I shall review the BT experience under the following headings, all of which are different aspects of the issues of efficiency and market structure: (*i*) the legal environment; (*ii*) entry and competition; (*iii*) vertical integration; and (*iv*) regulatory behaviour.

THE LEGAL ENVIRONMENT

The legal framework governing BT predates privatisation. There are two key documents — the Telecommunications Act, passed in April, 1984 and the twenty-five year licence granted to BT under that Act, which became effective in August, 1984.

The Act requires the appointment of a Director General of Telecommunications (DGT) and gives him power to set up the Office of Telecommunications (Oftel). The DGT is given general instructions under the Act, but there are some more specific guidelines — most notably, to promote the interests of consumers, effective competition and efficiency.

The Act prohibits unlicensed systems, with licences being granted by the Minister or the DGT with the other's advice or consent. Once a licence is granted, the DGT has the power to modify the conditions attaching to the licence and, very importantly, has the power to make reference to the Monopolies and Mergers Commission (MMC). If the MMC decides that certain practices are against the public interest and that the situation can be remedied by a modification of the licence conditions, the DGT can modify the conditions and can enforce compliance with the new conditions through the courts, who have ultimate power to revoke the licence.

The Act also of course provided for the ultimate privatisation of BT.

The Act does apparently give wide regulatory powers to the Minister, the DGT and the MMC, but these are very vaguely defined, and the extent to which regulation would be used with a pro-competitive emphasis would depend very much on how these people decided to exercise their functions. One suspects that one of the reasons why the Act is pretty vague on these things is that its contents were heavily influenced by BT itself, who clearly had an interest in minimising the possibility of competition.

One very significant feature of this legislation was that it did not provide for the break-up of BT. This is quite different from what is now being proposed by the British government as regards the electricity supply industry and from what happened in the US as regards telecommunications. As a result of an anti-trust case decided in 1982, AT & T was required to get rid of all its local networks (now run by 'Baby Bells'), though it kept its long-distance network and its equipment manufacturing activities from which the 'Baby Bells' are barred. So, there was a degree of both horizontal and vertical disintegration.

The other main element in the legal framework is the licence granted to BT. Two aspects of this are important for us.

The question of competition: The licence requires BT to connect other licensed systems to its own public network and the conditions under which this is done can be determined by the DGT. BT must not show undue preference to its own businesses, for instance in the supply or purchase of equipment. BT must not cross-subsidise things like apparatus supply or Value Added Networks (VANs) from other parts of its business, and it was required to set up separate accounts for its apparatus and network businesses. Various forms of discrimination among customers of apparatus or services are also prohibited.

The form of price control: there are two main issues here: (*i*) the price-control formula; and (*ii*) the range of application of that formula.

The British have chosen to use what they call the RPI-X formula and, for the five-year period ending in July, 1989, X was fixed at 3 — i.e. for the basket of services covered by the formula, BT's prices must not increase in any year by more than three percentage points less than the Retail Prices Index. There are two things worth noting about this:

(*a*) it is a direct prices formula, rather than the rate-of-return formula more favoured by American regulators. But this difference may be more apparent than real because the DGT has the power to apply for a variation in X and it is difficult to see how he could do that without reference to the rate of profit;

(*b*) the number 3 was arrived at by negotiation between BT and the relevant Ministry. It cannot be regarded as a very stringent constraint, given the pace of cost-reducing technical progress and of demand shift in this industry.

Also of concern is the range of application of this formula. Things like international calls, VAN, telex and call-boxes are excluded from the basket, whereas both local and long-distance domestic calls are included. This joint treatment of local and long-distance calls is of note, not only because it can accommodate high rates of increase in local-call charges, but also because it increases the capacity of BT to engage in predatory pricing in the only domestic competition facing it — with Mercury on long-distance networks.

ENTRY AND COMPETITION

With such a range of services and products at stake here, we could go on for ever. I shall therefore restrict my remarks to two areas: first, competition for BT as a network operator; and secondly, competition in equipment supply. (The latter is a question of the degree of vertical integration in this industry and I shall put it on one side for a moment.)

At present, and for the foreseeable future, there is only one national network operator in competition with BT: Mercury, a subsidiary of Cable and Wireless. Mercury obtained its initial licence in 1982, with a new licence being issued under the 1984 Act. Its public telephone service opened in 1986 and it is mainly associated with the business market. I want to make three points here:

(1) The British government has declared that no further licence will be issued until at least 1990. This ensures that BT and Mercury will remain a duopoly (though a very lop-sided one) for many years to come, and perhaps gives us one more clue as to the British government's true feelings about competition in the field of a former public enterprise of which it still owns nearly half the equity.

(2) The role of Oftel has been significant here. As already stated, both the Act and BT's licence require BT to provide interconnection with a licensed operator, the conditions of the interconnection to be determined by the DGT. These conditions are critical in determining the extent to which competition can exist. They cover not only the price charged for access to BT's network, but also things like routing. After an initial skirmish in 1985, when BT challenged the DGT's power to determine these conditions, Oftel ruled that the two networks must have full interconnection for international and domestic calls. Although the access charges could not exactly be described as marginal cost pricing, those charges are considerably less than BT would charge to one of its customers for a call. Mercury pays half the cost of new capacity required by BT to accommodate the interconnection. The fact that Oftel insisted on full interconnection, and set charges lower than average cost, is an indication of its general sympathy for competition.

(3) This is far from saying that there is genuine competition going on here. There was an initial flurry of leap-frogging price cuts for long-distance calls in the months following

May, 1986, when Mercury opened for business. This has settled down to a situation in which Mercury charges somewhat less than BT. There is no further competitor on the horizon and, since Mercury can be very profitable without doing much damage to BT's market-share, one might predict that this kind of semi-collusive duopoly will be maintained for the foreseeable future.

VERTICAL INTEGRATION

Vertical integration is of course a classic way of protecting one's core business. It only means that the battle lines are drawn elsewhere against different opposition, but this can be of considerable importance if the core business is subject to regulation which constrains one's commercial behaviour, but if the more peripheral business is subject to no such regulatory constraint. An episode of this type occurred in 1985, and it was significant because it showed the differences in attitude to competition of the three main actors on the regulatory stage: the Minister, the DGT and the MMC.

BT proposed to buy control of Mitel, a Canadian manufacturer of PABXs. BT did not make such equipment but, as the dominant supplier, it was the dominant buyer from manufacturers. At the time, Mitel had slightly under 20 per cent of the British PABX market, but it did have about half of the market for PABXs supplied by those other than BT. The matter was referred to the MMC. The DGT argued strongly before the MMC that the merger should either be disallowed or, if it were to be allowed, there should be a considerable strengthening of the regulatory regime. The MMC itself concluded that there was a general expectation that the merger would operate against the public interest, but recommended that it be allowed on condition that BT give certain undertakings (designed to prevent BT from using its relationship with Mitel to enhance its own equipment-supply business or to damage other producers or suppliers of equipment). The Minister allowed the merger, but the conditions he imposed were considerably less restrictive than those recommended by the MMC.

REGULATORY BEHAVIOUR

Regulatory quangos in the US have come in for a great deal

of criticism on the grounds that, allegedly, they have been too cosy with the firms they are supposed to regulate. One reason for this, if it is true, is asymmetric information. Regulation of a multi-product business requires the availability of complex accounting information of which the regulated firm is the only possible regular source. One cannot assume that, in dealing with the gamekeeper, the poacher will always act in good faith, and so the regulatory body will always be at a disadvantage.

Oftel is no different in this respect, but it has, unlike some US bodies, used its legal power to the very limit in requiring BT to change and disaggregate its accounting to enable Oftel to track performance *vis-à-vis* the requirements of the Act and the licence, and the conditions attached to the decisions relating to Mercury and Mitel. Two things have helped: first, BT tried to use its muscle against Oftel too early in the game (in relation to Mercury), thus causing the DGT to recognise that he had a classical monopolist on his hands; and secondly, the man appointed as the first DGT turned out to be an unreconstructed pro-competition enthusiast: Bryan Carsberg. Another point of relevance to Ireland is that Oftel is of a species unknown in this country: a regulatory body which is not part of a Ministry. This independence has been vital because Oftel and the DGT have been able to show publicly their difference of approach from that of the Minister and have been notably less protective of BT than has the Minister.

In my view, the BT experience tells us little about the merits or otherwise of privatisation as such, but it does tell us a great deal about regulation. When BT was in public hands, it was 'regulated' in the traditional way through the powers given to the Minister and the obligations imposed by the 1969 Act, which was a standard piece of public corporation legislation. In Ireland we are one stage behind in this process. Our equivalent of that British legislation is the Postal and Telecommunications Services Act of 1983. Although An Post and An Bord Telecom (as it was then, now with its name changed to Telecom Eireann) are established under the Companies Act, the 1983 legislation (aside from the parts to do with taking over the property of the Department of P & T) also looks very similar to legislation establishing statutory corporations — e.g. in giving the Minister powers to lay down policy guidelines, to vet price increases, and so on.

If the objective is efficiency, there is, with present technology, no immediate prospect of the privatisation of Irish domestic telecommunications or of a break-up *à la* AT & T. With a population of only 3.5 million, our national network has many of the characteristics of a local network elsewhere, and it is in local networks that unexhausted economies of scale most obviously exist. The 1983 Act itself gives Telecom Eireann the exclusive privilege of providing public telecommunications services (as the 1969 Act did for BT) and, in a very unusual and curiously worded Section 87(2), attempts to justify this monopoly power. It is unusual because it is rare for any legislation to include supportive arguments for its own provisions. It is curiously worded in the sense that one of the three arguments is a non-sequitur: that in 87(2)(a) which says that a monopoly is needed if a national service is to be profitable; and a second, that in 87(2)(c) underpins the counter-efficiency requirement in Section 51 that loss-making services which the Minister requires to be continued must be internally cross-subsidised from other services. The third refers to economies of scale, though not in such terms.

Although the Act does provide for the issue of licences to others (who may themselves be granted exclusive privileges) there is nothing in this legislation — and nothing in our long history of Ministerial relationships with public enterprises in the public utility area — to suggest that the kind of pressure which Oftel has kept up on BT would be replicated in this country. One can only live in hope that we in Ireland will use the British experience to recognise that non-Ministerial regulation, while (as the American experience has shown) not guaranteeing independence and continuous pressure to mitigate the effects of monopoly power does give opportunities for such desirable features which have much less hope of emerging in the traditional environment.

I am indebted to Dr Michael Mulreany of the Institute of Public Administration for his invaluable advice. He is not responsible for what I have done with that advice.

ENERGY AND PRIVATISATION IN IRELAND

Susan Scott

Economic and Social Research Institute

and

Frank J. Convery

University College, Dublin

INTRODUCTION
There are four state companies with a significant involvement in the energy field. These are the *Irish National Petroleum Company* (INPC) which operates an oil refinery at Whitegate; *Bord Gáis Eireann* (The Irish Gas Board, BGE) which has responsibility for gas distribution and for Dublin Gas; the *Electricity Supply Board* (ESB) which accounts for about one-third of primary energy consumption; and *Bord na Móna* which has responsibility for peatland development.

For each of these, we identify some of the issues involved in privatisation, and some general conclusions.

IRISH NATIONAL PETROLEUM COMPANY
This is an example of a special case: in contrast to the usual rationale for setting up state enterprises, one of the aims of INPC's establishment was the reduction of the perceived might of a private sector cartel. One could say that it was meant to improve efficiency and the level of competition. Its establishment also had two other objectives: to help the government to know what was going on and in particular to provide a more secure supply of oil by means of state-to-state deals.

The terminal and storage facilities at Whitegate near Cork enable the state company to import and hold an *average* of 200,000 tonnes of mainly crude oil, equivalent to about twenty days' national usage. This is a sizeable part of the ninety-day strategic store requirement. The refinery at Whitegate processes about one-third of the nation's petroleum needs but cannot usually produce at a competitive price. Its thirty-year-old technology produces an over-concentration of low-priced heavy product, and it is operated at about half capacity. INPC has no distribution outlets, so to ensure that INPC breaks even financially, the oil companies are obliged to source 35 per cent of their needs from Whitegate. This compulsory offtake adds to the consumer price of oil. In addition, it removes an incentive for INPC to become efficient. It should be noted that some small-scale refining is undertaken for third parties. INPC also owns a terminal at Whiddy, currently unusable, though the one million tonnes crude oil storage facility is intact. Planning permission is being applied for to restore the terminal. The Fair Trade Commission is at present reviewing aspects of the oil industry, including Whitegate pricing. Meanwhile, a Task force under the chairmanship of the Minister for Energy was established in May 1989 to identify all realistic options for upgrading the refinery and oil storage installations. Some £26 million has been earmarked to contribute to the upgrading, perhaps in a partnership deal. We can outline some of the options, and look at the potential for privatisation in each case.

The option of leaving the INPC without upgrading, i.e. to continue in its present form, is unrealistic. While the sourcing of crude oil by INPC does add an element of diversity to Ireland's oil supply, beyond this it is hard to see how the objectives of security and competition are fulfilled. In times of oil supply disruption, unless crude oil escapes the same disruption, the refinery would be idle. Whitegate would not be attractive to a private purchaser without the 35 per cent offtake requirement, while *with* the 35 per cent offtake the absence of incentive to achieve efficiency would defeat the intended efficiency gain of privatisation. The 35 per cent offtake rule would in any case be contrary to the spirit of the single European market, though it is not clear that the European Commission would be in a position to outlaw it.

Another option is to restructure INPC purely as a storage provider, possibly raising its capacity, such that it can maintain the entire ninety days' strategic supply. The storage of product being more costly than storage of crude, careful calculations of what is effectively an insurance measure need to be made, comparing its costs with alternative arrangements, including the current one. A different approach would be for the government to announce its intention to purchase a storage service, with Whitegate and Whiddy as facilities, and put this out to tender, on a five-yearly basis perhaps. In this manner security and competition might be combined. Independent non-strategic storage companies would appear to be unenthusiastic about the location of these facilities and there would appear to be no shortage of storage at present (*Petroleum Economist*, 1988).

Other options relating to the refinery have been mooted. A partnership with an oil-producing country is a possibility. Saudi Arabia, Kuwait, Venezuela, the UAE, Libya and Nigeria among others are interested in downstream activities, buying foreign refineries and petrol stations. This guarantees an outlet for their oil when markets are weak. This is also in the interest of oil-consuming countries, as it gives OPEC a vested interest in secure stable supplies. Kuwait, for example, now owns two refineries and 4,800 filling stations in Western Europe. A number of refineries are currently being upgraded to produce high octane output, now that lead is increasingly being replaced. In Western Europe refinery utilisation rates were 76 per cent in 1988 but in the UK, where there are many upgraded refineries, they have recently been operating at 95 per cent. Similarly, US refineries are operating at over 90 per cent. In the meantime, the world economic upturn, though moderating, still continues. Taking account of projects under way, world refinery capacity will increase by a modest 5 per cent by 1992, with most of this increase taking place in the Middle East (*Petroleum Economist*, 1989). There may therefore be scope for refinery operation in Ireland. Whitegate, however, would require some £70 to £220 million spent to upgrade the refinery. At full capacity it would supply some 65 per cent of national product needs. More would need to be spent if its size were to be increased severalfold in order to gain economies of scale, at which stage foreign markets would need to be found. Ireland does not have any special advantages as a location, which explains why Nigeria, one gathers, was mainly interested in Whitegate if a compulsory offtake were continued. State-to-state deals in petroleum with an oil-producing country, such as Russia, could secure good terms in so far as the producer is interested in limiting dependence on the major oil companies, but, with a more liberal overall world oil market emerging, Ireland would need to offer some special advantage. Privatisation would presumably not be an option if there is a state-to-state deal, the ability to gain such a deal being the rationale for state involvement.

A completely new outlook could be afforded by an oil find, conveniently situated and easily accessed. Investment in the refinery should then proceed if the product can broadly compete with imports, taking all costs into account. The INPC could be privatised with or without the investment in place.

In conclusion, it might be noted that in the US, where regulation of the oil market is very strong, oil prices net of tax and retail margins are estimated by the *Economist* (25 March 1989) at 20p per gallon cheaper than in Britain, where regulation is rather less strong. Meanwhile the UK Monopolies and Mergers Commission is investigating petrol retailing. Its report will be of some relevance to us. It might shed some light on the question whether the oil companies operating in these islands are or are not a cartel. If they are, then regulation should be considered. A privatised INPC would tend to join the cartel and obviously would also need to be subject to regulation. If the oil companies are not operating as a cartel, then some minimal effective supervision is still required to ensure that the situation continues.

BORD GÁIS EIREANN (BGE)

The privatisation of the British gas industry in December 1986 has provoked widespread criticism: for example (Robinson, 1989)

> The nadir of the [privatisation] programme so far was the privatisation of British gas; large numbers of people were tempted into becoming shareholders ... in an organisation which, if anything, had a more powerful monopoly position than its nationalised predecessor, since it had the

ability to diversify...

and, referring to the intended privatisation of electricity:

It would be a disaster for the community as a whole if there were another British Gas-style privatisation.

The market failure rationale for nationalising gas utilities had been that they were perceived to be natural monopolies. It makes little sense to have duplicate competing distribution pipeline systems. Vertical integration of transmission and distribution made coordination easier between purchase from producers (frequently oil companies), long-distance transmission, local distribution and sale to customers. Economies of scale implied declining long-run marginal costs (LRMC), requiring government subsidy if gas were priced at its LRMC, hence government involvement in supply, via nationalisation.

In practice, however, not all utilities operate as vertically integrated nationalised monopolies. In North America over two-thirds of gas flowing through long-distance pipelines is distributed for third parties, one-third of which is handled by marketing companies and brokers. Third parties are bodies which are neither gas producers nor pipeline owners and which, for example, purchase gas directly from a gas well and pay a fee for transmission. Also mitigating the natural monopoly argument is the fact that, in the medium term, gas customers can switch to other fuels — indeed some large industrial customers can and do switch in the short term, and are thereby able to exert considerable pressure on the supplier.

Whatever the arguments, British Gas (BG) was privatised without the reorganisation which would be required to induce competition. It provides gas under long-term contract from the exploration companies, transmits the gas to different parts of the country, distributes and sells it to customers, and sells and services gas appliances. Proposals to introduce competition with privatisation had been made but not adopted. For example, Hammond *et al.* (1985) had proposed dividing the industry into twelve independent companies for area distribution, with a further company operating the transmission. BG's existing relatively low-price contracts with the extraction companies would also be separated among the distribution companies. This would prevent British Gas, which in either case would operate the transmission network, from being able to undercut competitors. It would also create a market between companies extracting gas and companies distributing and selling gas to customers. The Office of Gas Supply (OFGAS) dispute this argument saying the existence of a few large suppliers would require the distribution companies to band together in any case (1987 Annual Report).

Because competition would put pressure on prices and profit margins, this latter approach is unlikely to have raised the £7.72 billion which the government in fact achieved from the sale, or to have resulted in such a large *number* of shareholders. It would have been less beneficial to the financial agents dealing with the flotation, and less beneficial to the unions and to BG management. Sir Dennis Rooke, the Chairman of British Gas, threatened to resign if 'his company' was vertically dismembered (Stelzer, 1989).

It was then up to OFGAS, the government-appointed gas regulatory body established in 1986, to ensure that the community did not suffer the market inefficiencies associated with monopolies. In particular, it would need to see that the entitlement of third parties or new entrants to use the BG pipeline was upheld, as laid down in the 1982 Oil and Gas (Enterprise) Act, reiterated in the 1986 Gas Act. If a third party is unsuccessful in negotiating use of the pipeline, it can apply to OFGAS who may issue a 'direction', carrying the weight of law, specifying the terms. These terms may also cover BG supply back-up charges.

The unfolding of the struggle between the privatised monopoly and its regulatory agency during the last three years makes interesting reading. OFGAS's first annual report is mild enough. It describes measures taken to get acquainted with the technical and commercial aspects of the industry, and seems to busy itself with safety issues and deposit levels, what short-stay gas customers should pay, and the like.

The second annual report starts talk of 'new challenges' and notes that no third party has availed of the right of access to the pipeline system. Factors expected to induce this type of competition, it says, included the unmet special needs of some large users and the prospects of new gas reserves, not committed to BG. OFGAS describes also some of the factors inhibiting competition. Being so large, BG is able to buy gas from the extraction companies at the onset of a field coming on stream, and for all the gas over the lifetime of the field. BG can offer reasonable take-or-pay terms, that is, it undertakes to make regular payment, even if it does not take up all its gas entitlement. It has a good record of honouring contracts, thereby reducing the suppliers' risk. OFGAS announced that it was ready to see that these risks were not unfairly loaded against the greater rewards of competition. Meanwhile, the Office of Fair Trading was particularly concerned about BG pricing to contract customers and referred BG to the Monopolies and Mergers Commission (MMC), enabling it also to investigate the situation with regard to third-party suppliers. There were still no applications to OFGAS in 1987 by third parties wishing to convey gas through the BG pipeline.

The MMC duly reported in October 1988 that BG practices 'extensive discrimination' against some big customers who had no alternative supply. In addition, it reported, third parties wishing to supply could be undercut by BG. Trade and Industry Secretary, Lord Young, subsequently introduced a measure which provides that 10 per cent of all future gas fields should be set aside for competitors to British Gas.

At this stage AGas, the first big potential competitor to British Gas, applied to use British gas pipelines. AGas is a company owned jointly by Associated Heat Services and Hadsons, the largest US independent gas marketing group. It intends to supply a combined heat and power plant in Manchester with gas bought from an independent North Sea producer, via BG's pipelines. Finding it hard to agree terms, AGas turned for assistance to OFGAS. This brings us to 17 May 1989 which saw a 'watershed for competition' in gas supply to large users, with OFGAS issuing a 'direction' to British Gas requiring it to open up its pipeline system to AGas. It is reported that AGas is trying to sign up gas supplies from five more North Sea producers and hopes to supply a tenth of the contract market within five years.

It may eventually be that the much criticised manner in which BG was privatised is, to some extent at least, self correcting. The regulatory framework in place was perhaps spurred into action by complaints at commentator and customer level. Ironically, it may be that the UK government will achieve most of its objectives in gas privatisation, *including* both competition and a flotation revenue, based on the assumption by investors that it would be a monopoly. But it is a method which one suspects can only work once. If such a monopoly were floated again, people may suspect that it will subsequently be 'undermined' by regulation.

Turning to the Irish scene, there are a few parallels as well as some special features. Bord Gáis Eireann (BGE) is a state monopoly purchaser of gas from Marathon, which in turn is currently a monopoly supplier of gas. There is no gas link to outside the island. BGE also has several subsidiary companies which are local distributors for Cork, Limerick and so on. Recently it has acquired Dublin Gas along with its bank debt of £62 million. Another important aspect of BGE is that its profits constitute the rent on the gas. This rent is transferred annually to the citizenry via the Exchequer.

If BGE were privatised, the sell-off price would effectively be the capitalised value of this future revenue stream. This might have worked out at between say £700 million and £900 million, based on the 1985 profit and assuming people thought its monopoly status would stay intact (Convery, 1987). The figure would be somewhat lower now, since the takeover of Dublin Gas though, as we shall discuss, this situation may revert. It has to be said that such a flotation would involve the government in a considerable gamble because they would have to make a judgment about future oil prices, the dollar, the economy and inflation, among other things. But then this is just the counterpart of the very uncertain revenue stream in the current situation.

BGE's contract with Marathon, as with mid-1970s contracts elsewhere, is on favourable terms relative to contracts today. On its sales, BGE can in theory determine the price it charges to specific customers, subject to general guidelines laid down by government. However, it is evident from annual reports that NET (who sell on to Irish Fertiliser Industries) is charged a price which is below the price that present and future potential customers would be willing to pay, notably the ESB. If this pricing arrangement did not survive privatisation, its removal could perhaps add considerably to the capitalised value of BGE. The government would then need to consider giving an overt subsidy to Irish Fertiliser Industries, if the latter is to survive.

Some of the urban distribution companies might be candidates for potential privatisation. Dublin Gas might not be such a candidate at present, though if the momentum of the current sales drive continues, with its debts cleared, its new central heating customers reverting to full-price gas (that is double the present promotional price they are paying) in two or three years' time, and with some help from a pick-up in the economy, the outlook might be transformed.

An 'alternative' British Gas privatisation proposal suggested that the regional distribution companies inherit the existing low-price contracts agreed with the extraction companies. It is not clear that this can be accommodated under the Irish Gas Act of 1976 which effectively gives BGE first refusal on gas extracted from areas under Irish jurisdiction. Part V, section 37, of the Act provides that

> all natural gas landed in the State ... for consumption therein, by the licensee under an exploration licence or the lessee of a petroleum lease shall be offered for sale to the Board on reasonable terms [except where] the Minister for Industry and Commerce, in approving a plan for the development or exploitation of a deposit of natural gas, requires [it] to be offered for sale to a person, other than the Board, for an industrial purpose specified in the requirement.

So, BGE might not let others purchase new finds, let alone transfer the Kinsale contract. Short of making Kinsale gas available to other companies, and the legislation entailed, there is no ready solution. The Act might not need amendment for third parties to be able, legally, to purchase new finds from the extraction companies. However, British experience suggests that BGE, having first refusal, would buy it up unless an industrial purpose had been specified in the development or exploitation plans. Something like the UK 10 per cent rule might be the answer.

The Irish Gas Act is vague on imports of gas, but third parties on their own would not have sufficient sales for this to be a financially viable source. No private company has shown interest in importing to the Northern Ireland market in the preclosure years, as far as one can gather. However, among other imponderables, it is not clear that British Gas would have been willing to sell to such a private company.

Where use of the transmission system is concerned, British experience also suggests that a strong regulation framework needs to be in place, supported perhaps by consumer sentiment. There may be a presumption in the Irish Gas Act, as quoted above, that gas from extraction companies required directly by the Minister to go to an 'industrial purpose specified' could be required to be transmitted by the Irish Gas pipeline system, but again this is vague and untested. As we saw, the British amended their law to give entitlement to use the transmission system, in the 1982 Act.

More recently, it should be noted, the European Commission has passed a draft directive on the transmission of gas through major systems. This proposes that pipeline owners be required to allow other utilities to avail of the pipeline, or 'common carriage'. A report by consultants, Coopers and Lybrand/Belmont prepared for the Commission points out, however, that

> those member states which have still to build up their basic gas industry infrastructure might find that the uncertainty created by a common carriage right for large industrial consumers makes it very difficult to finance the substantial investments required in the early phases of gas development.

The consultants therefore propose a 'temporary exemption from the full common carriage system for states such as Greece, Ireland, Portugal and Spain' (FT International Gas Report, 1989).

To conclude, we have seen there are several areas of uncertainty, particularly in relation to the power of BGE. In any event, a privatised transmission system which was open for transmission of third party gas would be unlikely to promote efficiency gains in the absence of more potential suppliers. The market is set to expand with the pipeline extension programme (National Development Plan 1989-93). On the other hand, potential suppliers may not be emerging because they currently have to deal with BGE, a monopoly buyer. It is sometimes argued that a link to the British gas grid could alter the situation by giving access to many potential purchasers, especially under the new, more competitive regime there. Alternatively, one could argue the other way. There has been increased talk recently about the building of a link with the UK or the Continent for the purchase of gas when Kinsale is depleted, culminating in a proposal in the National Development Plan conditional on the economies of the link. Coincidentally, there was Marathon's announcement of the new offshore gas find off Ballycotton. This delays the need for the link and thereby maintains Marathon's status as a monopoly supplier for a while longer. What encouraged the find was probably the improved terms agreed with exploration companies. Whichever way one argues, the present gas industry, though dominated by monopolies, is trying to gain market share and faces competition from other fuels in most of its energy markets: space heat, process heat, cooking and so on. BGE is therefore already under pressure to operate efficiently. Privatisation as it stands would mainly affect how BGE allocates its sales. Legislative changes and regulation could enable third parties to buy from exploration companies and use the transmission lines. However, the theoretical ideal of a market which is opened up, with many potential suppliers and buyers, is unlikely to be attained without a link with another gas grid, if then. In turn, such a link needs to be justified on economic, security and environmental grounds.

ELECTRICITY SUPPLY BOARD
The benefits and costs of privatisation depend in part on how it is to be effected. Three approaches can be distinguished:

Disposal as a vertically integrated utility: The ESB is a vertically integrated utility, buying its own fuel, generating electricity, distributing it through the grid to customers. Under disposal without restructuring, this company would be sold as is, in whole or in part.

Before investors would be willing to invest, the following would have to be clarified:

(1) *How and to what extent the company's non-commercial responsibilities would be discharged.* About 15 per cent of the ESB's output is provided from generating stations burning peat. This is expensive relative to the least-

cost alternative available at the margin (heavy fuel oil). This 'costs' the ESB, and therefore electricity consumers, in the order of £25-£50 million annually, the exact amount depending on oil prices and how fixed costs are allocated. The benefits of this transfer occur in the form of the substantial employment and income generated in the Midlands, via the peat development, harvesting and transport activities of Bord na Móna. (The situation *vis-á-vis* Bord na Móna is changing as will be seen below).

(2) *How decisions on electricity prices will be made*. At present, the price which is arrived at is a product of negotiations between the ESB and the government. Broadly speaking, as long as electricity prices are falling in real terms — as at present — and are not significantly out of line with UK levels, then price agreement is readily reached. The Department of Energy and its institutional predecessors do not appear to have invested significantly in the economic, financial and technical skills and data which would allow them to arrive at independent judgments about the appropriateness or otherwise of price proposals. However, when real price increases are in prospect, and/or when Irish electricity prices move out of line with the European average, then consumer and ultimately political pressure builds up. An analogous situation to that which we recently experienced with regard to petrol prices can arise, when the government has a direct interest in keeping prices down, while the oil industry argues that this can only be accomplished if losses are to be incurred. An investigation or Commission is established which examines and reports accordingly. The latest such exercise which has been published *vis-á-vis* electricity is the *Report of the Inquiry into Electricity Prices* (Department of Energy, Dublin, 1984).

In the eve.it of privatisation, this informal, highly unstructured approach would in all likelihood have to be replaced by a more formal system. The framework used in the US to regulate private vertically integrated utilities represents the apogee — or nadir (depending on one's point of view) — of this formal approach: the utility is entitled to a 'reasonable' rate of return on investment, while the regulator demands that the utility produce electricity as cheaply as possible. In practice, a very adversarial situation has developed. Take the situation where a utility is judged by some to have made a poor investment decision, e.g. in relation to a nuclear power plant, and then seeks a rate increase to give it a 'reasonable' rate of return on that investment. Should these costs be passed through? If not, how is the utility to attract new investment capital? What is the definition of a 'poor' investment? Is a utility not entitled to make any mistakes? In addition to such 'commercial' questions, regulators must deal with issues such as environment and energy conservation. There is statutory provision for public input and involvement, and a highly adversarial pattern has emerged, whereby the utility is accused of inefficiency and incompetence, and the utility in turn complains of being asked to achieve the impossible with rates of return which are not competitive.

In all such debates, there will tend to be an asymmetry in the nature and quality of the information available. The utility will have precise information on its costs and markets, but will have an incentive not to make this available to the regulator, who cannot be as informed.

The *benefits* of vertically integrated privatisation are as follows:

(*a*) *The initial Exchequer benefit*: According to accounting convention, the proceeds of a sale are treated as a revenue receipt. Set against this are the net earnings which would have accrued to the government if the ESB had remained in public ownership. Since market values reflect future as well as current earnings, there is a net revenue gain in the year of sale.

How large is the gross sale value likely to be? Three experts valued the ESB independently in 1987 as follows (Convery, 1987):

	Value (Millions of 1987£)
Expert I	500
Expert II	420
Expert III	550
Average	490

The cost of promoting and underwriting issues in the UK have fallen in the range of 3-6 per cent of the issue value, and in order to ensure success in a number of cases, the subscription price has been set well below the share 'market' value (Mayer and Meadowcroft, 1985).

(*b*) *More transparency in policy objectives and rate setting*: It seems likely that prospective investors will demand that the regulatory framework be well defined as to objectives and procedures before they commit their money. Specifically — in the light of the experience of oil companies this year in relation to oil prices — they will want to know how fuel price rises will be passed through, and how gains in productivity will be distributed.

(*c*) *Easier access to equity capital*: Given the small, open nature of the Irish economy, there is a strong *a priori* case for investing in utility and related investments in other countries. The ESB has paid for its system out of earnings and borrowings. It is difficult at the best of times to get capital from the shareholder (the Irish government); it would probably be impossible to get equity from the state to finance acquisitions overseas, while it would be more feasible for a private company to do so.

There is a worldwide trend towards privatisation which will yield opportunities in this regard.

The costs of vertically integrated privatisation are as follows:

(*a*) *Foregone future earnings*: Because of the ESB's high borrowings and therefore interest payments, the pressure to keep down prices, and a conservative accounting convention, the surplus/deficit over 1982-8 period ranged from minus £22 million in 1984 to plus £7 million in 1982. However, with the bulk of its generating capacity in place, burning a good range of fuels, of which two — coal and gas — are very competitively priced, the ESB could have some profitable years ahead. These returns will be foregone by privatisation.

(*b*) *Maintenance of monopoly power*: Monopoly in electricity derives from the control of the grid. When a vertical monopoly is privatised, this monopoly power remains intact. There is unlikely to be any gain in efficiency resulting from privatisation. It is possible that private monopoly would in the long run behave less efficiently than a public monopoly, because the altruistic dimension will be less salient.

(*c*) *Complex regulatory framework*: The transparency of objectives and procedures were listed as an advantage. A possible parallel disadvantage is that the arms length requirement may engender procedural requirements which cause frustration and inefficiency.

(*d*) *Strategic concerns*: A privatised company can also be taken over by another company, something which the Single European Act facilitates. When the ESB was established in 1927, the decision to keep electricity generation and distribution in state hands was made on the basis that electricity was an essential commodity which should not be monopolised under private control. Given the plethora of public, cooperative and private electricity companies which have operated successfully since then throughout the world over several decades, this view is perhaps not as salient as before; but it will weigh in the political calculations.

Privatisation with separation of generation and distribution: Monopoly power has to be exercised only at the stage of distribution. Generation can readily be undertaken at a variety of locations, using various fuels and generation systems under different ownerships.

In its decision to privatise the electricity business in England and wales, the British government decided to separate generation from distribution. The proposal is as follows: twelve private distribution companies will buy power from two private generating companies. The Central Electricity Generating Board (CEGB) will be split up into three companies: National Power, known as Big G, will own 70 per cent of CEBG's generating capacity, including the nuclear stations. Implicitly, Big G is being given quasi-monopoly power so that it can afford to carry the nuclear capacity. The Power Generation Company, known as Power Gen or as Little G, will own the remainder (30 per cent). The National Grid Company will own the national grid, the transmission links with France and Scotland and the Dinorwig pumped storage station. It will be up to the Area Boards to secure supplies. An independent agency — the Office of Electricity Supply (OFELECT) — will have regulatory powers. Up to 10 per cent of the electricity supplied to the Area Boards should come from sources other than Big G and Little G (the Southeast Electricity Board — Seaboard — have already commissioned feasibility studies in this regard:

Financial Times, 18 May 1989). The new generating companies are to be freed from their requirement to purchase from the British Coal Board.

It seems likely that a price formula linking the rate of increase of charges to the retail price index (RPI), minus X to represent the expected cost savings, plus the pass-through of unavoidable inputs (Y), (i.e. allowable increase = RPI-X+Y) will be used.

As noted above, there is already a requirement that one of the generating companies 'carry' nuclear power. On 15 May 1989, the House of Lords approved a new clause in the Bill which would enable penalties to be imposed on any privatised electricity suppliers failing to promote energy efficiency measures (reported in the *Independent*, 17 May 1989, p. 10). These interventions highlight the important non-market dimensions involved.

The costs and benefits associated with privatisation with separation of generation and distribution will be the same as for vertical privatisation, with one important difference: the former is designed to allow and indeed to encourage competition, while the latter is not.

However, it seems unlikely that two companies will compete with each other in any substantive fashion. The provision for new entrants — providing up to 10 per cent of the total electricity — is however likely to put some pressure on existing suppliers.

If a larger number of generating companies had been established, then competition would be more likely.

It is difficult to judge how feasible it would be in the Irish context to split generation from distribution, and to further divide the former into a number of generating companies. It may be indicative of the scale issue that the two Scottish companies are not being divided horizontally; they are being privatised as integrated companies.

Formalising access to the grid by private producers: Under this approach, access to the grid is 'privatised' by allowing companies to build generating capacity for supply to the system. Experience shows that when decisions on pricing and volume are left to a state or private vertical monopoly, very little 'private' electricity is taken. As noted earlier, under the

British government proposals, a proportion of the grid space must be kept for 'outside' suppliers. This is one way of introducing a degree of competition, and privatising some of the grid-carrying capacity.

Conclusions on electricity. We conclude that privatisation of the Electricity Supply Board would raise a substantial sum — in the range of £500 million to £1000 million — with the amount depending on the form the privatisation took. There is a tradeoff between maximising the sale price and the encouragement of efficiency and competition: if it is sold as a vertical monopoly, revenue will be greater than if it is disposed of on the basis that some competition will be allowed.

The potential benefits of privatisation are twofold: the private company would be able to raise capital, to fund domestic investments and for the acquisition of overseas capacity. Its management would be freer of 'political' interference — the pressure to keep particular stations open, to buy particular fuels, to supply particular categories of customers at concessionary rates. In Table 1 the fuel costs and works cost per unit for the generating stations in the ESB system are shown. However, because of the monopolistic nature of the industry, a strong regulatory regime *vis-à-vis* price is inevitable. Because of the role of strategic and environmental considerations, the regulatory brief is very likely to extend to other areas. We have seen already in the UK that the 'pure' privatisation process has been compromised by the government in the interests of maintaining nuclear capacity, and the regulatory system will have powers and responsibilities which extend beyond a concern with prices and competition. Thus a private Irish utility company will not be able to escape the regulatory/political dimension, although the latter may be more overt and predictable.

We conclude as follows:
— the nature and quality of the regulatory system would have a critical bearing on the desirability or otherwise of privatisation;
— privatisation without competition is unlikely to result in efficiency gains;

Table 1

Stations ranked by Work Costs per Unit

Station	Rank 1987 (1979)	Fuel Type	Fuel cost per Unit Sent Out (P)	Capacity NW	Plant load Factor (%)	Other Non-Capital Costs per Unit Sent out	Work Costs per Unit
Cliff and Kathleen's Falls	1 (1)	Hydro	–	65	44	0.556	0.5
Ardnacrusha	2 (2)	Hydro	–	86	40	1.046	1.0
Clady	3 (5)	Hydro	–	4	44	1.239	1.2
Carrigadrohid Inniscarra	4 (3)	Hydro	–	27	32	1.299	1.2
Moneypoint	5 (–)	Imported	1.293	915	67.6	0.3	1.5
Poolaphuca Golden Falls Leixlip	6 (4)	Hydro	–	38	11	2.129	2.1
Aghada	7 (–)	Natural	2.074	525	50.3	0.405	2.4
North Wall	8 (–)	Gas/Oil	2.011	146	45.5	0.552	2.58
Poolbeg	9 (10)	Gas/Oil	1.948	510	36.2	0.633	2.58
Tarbert	10 (11)	Oil	1.982	500	21.3	0.952	2.93
Marina	11 (6)	Gas	2.030	115	25.9	1.781	3.87
Lanesboro	12 (7)	Milled Peat	3.098	85	58.5	0.877	3.97
Ferbane B	13 (–)	Milled Peat	3.489	30	70.8	1.126	4.67
Shannonbridge	14 (8)	Milled Peat	3.603	125	48.2	1.017	4.62
Great Island	15 (14)	Oil	2.235	120	13.1	2.733	4.96
Ferbane A	16 (12)	Milled Peat	4.282	60	44.3	1.392	5.67
Rhode A	17 (9)	Milled Peat	4.181	40	24.1	2.504	6.68
Arigna	18 (19)	Domestic Coal	5.328	15	50.8	2.113	7.44
Allenwood	19 (16)	Sod Peat	3.946	40	16.4	4.31	8.25
Bellacorick	20 (15)	Milled Peat	3.729	40	18.9	4.667	8.39
Portarlington	21 (17)	Sod Peat	4.402	12	23.0	6.61	11.01
Cahirciveen Gweedore Screeb	22 (20)	Sod Peat	5.918	15	8.8	16.307	22.22

— we will have the inestimable benefit of actual UK privatisation experience to study and learn from. Within about three years it should indicate whether this model does in fact yield lower cost electricity. If it does, we will have little choice but to follow the same path.

BORD NA MÓNA

Bord na Móna is the state company established to develop Ireland's peat bogs. On economic efficiency grounds, there are two reasons why the state should have been involved: there have been substantial economies of scale in peat development. This required large expanses of bog, which in turn required powers of compulsory acquisition. Secondly, the technology of large-scale peat extraction under Irish conditions was undeveloped, making it a high-risk venture which at the time only the state was likely to undertake.

A distributional concern emerged subsequently, whereby Bord na Móna became a very important source of employment in the Midlands.

At present, the rationale for state involvement is less compelling, in that the most exploitable bogs have already been acquired, and technological development has allowed small bog development to proceed commercially, albeit with grant aids. However, the social role in the Midlands remains.

The current core activities of Bord na Móna can be grouped as follows: moss peat and horticultural services, domestic fuel supply (briquettes), fuel supply for electricity generation, and miscellaneous activities. Table 2 gives a sense of the turnover in the various areas.

We have no official data on the separate net returns in these activity areas. However, some insights and intuitions can be provided. The peat for power generation, although a core business in terms of resource use, sales volume and employment, is only profitable in most years because the price paid for peat by the ESB is higher — often substantially higher — than the price of the least cost alternative.

For 1987, the extent of the 'subsidy' ranged from £20 million to £50 million, depending on the treatment of relatively fixed plant costs (i.e. whether the peat-using plants were closed down or not — Table 3). With the exception of the years of very high oil prices, a subvention in the form of

Table 2

Value of Output, by Activity, 1987, £ million

ACTIVITY	TOTAL VALUE	%
Peat for Power Generation	62.3	54
Briquettes	25.1	22
Moss Peat and Horticulture	21.9	19
Miscellaneous	6.7	5
Total	116.0	100

Source: Bord na Móna Annual Report, 1987-8.

a 'high' price for the fuel has been necessary. Note however that some stations are close to being competitive, while others are dramatically the reverse.

Briquettes comprise a popular domestic fuel, manufactured from milled peat. They compete without benefit of price support — in fact their price was controlled below the market-clearing level for many years. Briquettes may secure a greater market share in Dublin in future, as a result of the banning of bituminous coal, because briquettes qualify as a smokeless fuel. Data on profitability by activity are not publicly available, but the moss peat and horticulture activity appears to be profitable, with a substantial export business operating in a growing market, with a high quality product.

Other activities include loose turf sales, consulting, and the development of new products and uses. The latter involves the use of peat in sewage treatment, the filtering out of contaminants etc; some of these developments show considerable promise.

Issues in privatisation: Clearly, the business of supplying peat to power stations is not one which could be sold in the conventional sense, unless production costs were reduced, and/or if any appropriate long-term contract with the ESB was part of the package.

Bord na Móna and its staff have decided to tackle the production cost problem by having some of the production staff form a number of companies (in which Bord na Móna has a minority stake) to produce milled peat. These companies will be free to diversify into other activities. It is likely that this will result in lower costs. It is not clear how, or to what extent, these savings will be passed through. If the transfer price of milled peat falls, this will improve the viability of the ESB peat-using stations, and of the briquette and other domestic fuel business.

Having created autonomous units for the production of peat, it seems likely that the more dynamic of these new entities will start developing additional activities, take out leases on new bogland, start competing perhaps in the logic in emulating the approach in other areas.

Except for the supply of peat for electricity generation, Bord na Móna must sell into very competitive markets. A key

Table 3

Fuel Cost Saving and Maximum In-Plant Non-Fuel Savings by Transferring Output to Tarbert, 1987

Station	Rank	Units sent out in 1987 (million)	Fuel Cost per Unit (P)	Saving per Unit (P)	Fuel Cost Saving million £	Max. Non-Fuel Cost Saving million £	Totals
Cahirciveen Gweedore Screeb	22	9.8	5.918	3.936	0.194	1.598	1.79
Portarlington	21	21.3	4.402	2.42	0.515	1.408	1.92
Bellacorick	20	61.0	3.729	1.747	1.066	2.85	3.91
Allenwood	19	53.2	3.945	1.963	1.044	2.293	3.33
Arigna	18	63.2	5.328	3.346	2.115	1.335	3.45
Rhode A	17	77.9	4.181	2.199	1.713	1.951	3.66
Ferbane A	16	213.5	4.282	2.3	4.910	2.972	7.88
Great Island	15	129.8	2.235	0.253	0.328	3.547	3.87
Shannonbridge	14	483.2	3.603	1.621	7.833	4.914	12.74
Ferbane B	13	175.9	3.489	1.507	2.651	1.981	4.63
Lanesboro	12	401.7	3.098	1.116	4.483	3.523	8.00
		1690.5			26.852	28.372	55.224

horticultural area, etc. Having released this particular genie from the bottle, if it proves successful there will be a certain requirement for success will be access to equity to help take advantage of opportunities, both domestically and overseas. Partial or total privatisation is one way of raising such equity. The advantages of such a development are clear. The disadvantages are perhaps a certain loss of identity between the state and peat development, and a loss of control *vis-à-vis* the achievement of political and regional development objectives.

GENERAL COMMENTS AND CONCLUSIONS
(1) If short-term generation of revenue for the Exchequer is a critically important objective, then the ESB and BGE are the prime candidates for privatisation in the energy field. The more complete the monopoly power which is transferred to the private sector with them the greater the Exchequer gain.
(2) A transfer of 'complete' monopoly power to the private sector is unlikely to improve operational cost-effectiveness, and may make matters worse in this regard as a net revenue-maximising ethos replaces a less coherent but welfare-oriented set of objectives. However, privatisation would facilitate the raising of equity capital, and the financing of acquisitions, and is likely to reduce the degree of political involvement in decision making. If this is accompanied by a form of privatisation which does introduce some competition, then efficiency is likely to be enhanced, but the revenue raised from the sale is likely to be reduced. The nature and quality of the regulatory process will determine in part whether competition is encouraged and efficiency is enhanced or not.
(3) In Britain, British Gas was privatised with its monopoly powers intact. However, in a directive of 17 May 1989, the regulatory body (OFGAS) ordered that a private company buying gas from an independent North Sea producer and wishing to supply a combined heat and power plant in Manchester be allowed to use British Gas pipelines. Earlier, it was announced that 10 per cent of all future gas fields should be set aside for competitors to British Gas. In this case, competition is being introduced after privatisation has taken place.

In the case of the electricity privatisation now being considered by the UK Parliament, it is hoped to induce competition by separating distribution from generation, by dividing the latter into two companies, and by allowing access to the grid (up to 10 per cent) to other generators (including those owned by the distributing companies).

It is essential to monitor UK experience carefully, and learn the right lessons; if it does work, we could quite suddenly find ourselves again in Ireland very exposed as the gap between our costs and British costs widens in their favour. The experience in N. Ireland and Scotland should be especially relevant.

(4) Since the *raison d'être* of the Irish National Petroleum Company (INPC) is in part to facilitate state-to-state deals, privatisation would undermine this function. In addition, its production costs are such that it is unlikely to have a significant market value to prospective investors unless the requirement on the part of the oil companies to take 35 per cent of the offtake were to be continued. (The Minister for Energy has indicated that about £26 million will be spent upgrading the refinery at Whitegate; this would enhance marketability somewhat.)

(5) Bord na Móna is pioneering a new approach to its lack of competitiveness in peat production, by having production workers form small companies which will supply peat to the Board's outlets. The full or partial privatisation of some of the other activities of the Board would provide equity capital. Given the borrowings of the company, and the government's restrictive policy regarding public expenditure, partial or full privatisation of some of its activities should be seriously considered. Unless the borrowing burden is reduced and additional capital is invested, it will be difficult for the Board to capitalise on its initiatives in product and market development, and on the anticipated fall in its production costs.

(6) Environmental impacts are inseparable from the extraction, production, transport and consumption of energy. Oil spills at sea, global warming, acid rain, habitat destruction, smoke pollution, strip mining, lead in the atmosphere, are just a few of the contemporary associations between energy and environment. Environmental

management can be defined as the breaking of the link between energy production and consumption, and environmental impact.

What are the implications for the environment of privatisation? The following are among the issues which arise in the context of the four state companies under discussion:

— emissions of sulphur from coal- and oil-fired electricity generating plants, and the implications for acid rain;
— emissions of CO_2 from all fossil fuel combustion, and the implications for global warming;
— loss of unique habitat, as a result of exploitation of virgin peat;
— role of natural gas in improving air quality in Dublin.

It is clear from US experience and from our own that very demanding environmental requirements can be imposed on private companies. An issue of compensation might however arise if the environmental rules were significantly changed after a privatisation had taken place. For example, if the ESB's very cost-effective coal-burning plant at Moneypoint were privatised, and subsequently the government decided that sulphur emissions should be eliminated therefrom, this would impose very substantial capital and operating costs. Investors might argue that they are entitled to compensation if they are not allowed or able to 'pass through' all of the costs to consumers. However, such ex-post environmental restrictions are likely to increase; prospective investors in energy activities will need to be aware of this.

NOTES

3: PROMISES AND PITFALLS

1. In addition, the US has implemented extensive deregulation programmes in transport and finance. Although privatisations and deregulations tend to be lumped together in public discourse, as policy options they are very different from each other. This is particularly apparent when we look at the options a public enterprise makes available to the skilful politician; a public enterprise is a vehicle through which policies can be carried out, while regulation can only set guidelines within which firms carry out their own policies. The basic model of reference developed in section two does not readily lend itself to the regulatory environment.

2. In recent years, the big increases occur in the specialised service and large-scale research and technology sector. The relevant figures can be found in the CEEP Handbook, published by the CEEP in Brussels.

3. This statement, admittedly, neither does justice to the complex process leading to the consolidation of the rail companies, nor to the political processes finally leading to the sale of ConRail.

4. See for example Boorsma, P.B., *Privatisering*, 1984.

5. See for example Bös, *Public Enterprise Economics*, 1986, ch. 1.4.

6. See for example, Backhaus and Wagner, 1987.

7. With the exception of the Austrian writers, perhaps. Note that Mises wrote *Die Gemeinwirtschaft (Economic Calculation under Socialism)* in order to show that under the conditions of a socialist regime, efficient economic allocation could not be achieved. This does not imply that public enterprises operating in a market economy have to

be inefficient by virtue of their being public.

8. For a survey see Backhaus, 1976.

9. See for example Backhaus, 1977 and 1980, part C.

10. See for example Blankart, 'Eléments', 1987.

11. The theory of the second best developed from an initial question about optimal pricing for a public enterprise delivering raw materials to an oligopolistically organised private industry.

12. The German term is 'Gemeinwirtschaft', most of this literature can be found in a specialised journal, *Zeitschrift für öffentliche und gemeinwirtschaftliche Unternehmen.*

13. See for example Backhaus, 1977 and 1980, as well as Friedmann, 1972.

14. For the UK, Lord Morrison's proposals of a 'public corporation' are typical. See Backhaus, 1977 and 1980, part G IV, and Musolf, 1983.

15. No doubt, this is a very crude approach. It may be sufficient for this basic discussion.

16. The need for this purpose becomes the more urgent as parliamentary control of government increases in effectiveness. Many public enterprises are off budget or appear in the annual budget only according to the net principle. This implies that public enterprise conduct is often subject to considerably less parliamentary scrutiny than governmental administrative agencies. If a particular administration is exposed to adverse parliamentary scrutiny, it will therefore be inclined to use public enterprises in order to carry out delicate and politically controversial policies. This discussion may not be relevant to some developing countries such as India which follow different procedures (I am unable to document them at this time).

17. This is a special case of *usus fructus.* Consequently, Steven Cheung's theory of share tenance become basically applicable, with a special twist. While the share tenant cannot always expect to regain tenancy, in the case of a non-continuation of his contract he does not have to turn the land over to an opponent.

18. This discussion is in the spirit of McCormick and Tollison, 1981.

19. This is why we observe tenured appointments in

government enterprises, when untenured appointments are the practice in comparable private enterprises After privatisation, cost reductions tend to occur in the personnel budget.

20. With respect to the emphasis on the establishment of profitable enterprises, the difference between those countries that followed mercantilist policies and those that implemented the cameralist programmes is striking. While earlier data are either incomplete or unreliable, there are relatively reliable data for the second half of the nineteenth century. These show the considerably greater extent to which the leading central European states with huge military establishments, such as the Prussian kingdom, were able to finance their activities predominantly from entrepreneurial ventures into such activities as agriculture and railways. For instance, Eheberg (1900) notes that for various dates in the early 1880s net income from state agricultural enterprises comprised 1.5 per cent of state revenues in France, 3 per cent in England, 3.6 per cent in Russia, and 3.9 per cent in Austria-Hungary. But the corresponding figure for Prussia was 16.4 per cent. For roughly the same period, Rimpler (1900:200) cites Adolf Wagner as finding that the net income from state agricultural enterprises provided 7.1 per cent of state revenues in Baden, 9.7 per cent in Saxony, 13.2 per cent in Württemberg, and 17.3 per cent in Bavaria. But the same numbers were only 4.1 per cent in Switzerland, 3.6 per cent in Greece, 3.4 per cent in Russia, 3 per cent in Italy, 2.9 per cent in Denmark, 1.9 per cent in the Netherlands, 1.4 per cent in France, 1.2 per cent in Norway, 1 per cent in Belgium, 0.6 per cent in England and Portugal, and 0.5 per cent in Austria. Agricultural enterprises were, of course, steadily declining throughout the Western world as a source of state revenue. But some states, principally German, looked to the development of new enterprises to replace the declining agricultural revenues, while others did not, and looked to taxation instead. Railways were of particular importance in this regard. According to Eheberg (1900), the share of state revenues produced by agricultural enterprises fell during the nineteenth century in Prussia

from 26.7 per cent in 1805 to 13.3 per cent in 1850 to 3.2 per cent in 1898-9. However, whereas the net income from railways provided only 2.5 per cent of Prussia's revenues in 1850, it provided 15.6 per cent in 1861 and 43.6 per cent in 1898-9. For the budgetary year 1896-7, the net income from various Prussian state enterprises provided 56.8 per cent of Prussia's revenues. And state enterprises were likewise important sources of revenue in the other industrially advanced states in the federation. For instance, the comparable figures for 1896-7 were 59.5 per cent for Saxony, 47.7 per cent for Württemberg, and 30.7 per cent for Bavaria (Eheberg: 923). And even the newly formed empire (i.e., federation) itself, whose only enterprise was the postal service, was able to finance 5.6 per cent of its budget from its lone enterprise. Finally, and to give an example where the concern for efficiency bears fruit only in the long run, net revenues from state forests per hectare in 1987 were (in marks) 42.91 in Württemberg, 41.42 in Baden, 26.5 in Alsace-Lorraine, and 15.99 in Saxony.

21. In a different context, this point was earlier made by Goldscheid, 1917.

22. Note that this effect is the exact opposite of the Averch'/Johnson effect which occurs under certain regulatory regimes (when the costs of capital determine rate increases).

23. The proceeds from the sale of public enterprises should not be taken as measure of the entire political gain. When sales price is accepted that lies below the value of the firm, the difference can be used for political ends, as when particular income groups receive shares at a discount.

24. 'Age' is, of course, but one example. Public services can be tailored to fit most any social group.

25. This argument is originally due to Amilcare Puviani (1960) who introduced the creation of illusory government performance systematically into public finance analysis.

26. See for example Backhaus, 1977 and 1980, part G III.

27. See for example Edelman, 1977.

28. Instead, the federal government supported Chrysler without taking it over.

29. During the World Economic Crisis, three major Italian banks (Banco di Roma, Banco Commerciale, and Credito Italiano) became insolvent and were taken over by the state. Their vast stock portfolios, inadvertently acquired by the state, where incorporated into the holding IR1 (Instituto per la Ricostruzione Industriale) by decree of May 1933.
30. The item is absent from all the public finance text books I have surveyed with the exception of Stiglitz, 1988.
31. Her Majesty's treasury privatisation in the United Kingdom background briefing 1987.
32. Bruno Molitor, 'Vermögenspolitik'. *Handwörterbuch der Wirtschaftswissenschaft 8*, 1980, 282-299 (287-288). Molitor reviews the German experience mostly during the sixties and early seventies and pleads for the distribution of shares in holding companies which, in turn, hold the stock of the privatised companies. The main idea behind this proposal is that the newly initiated stockholders should own shares that are less subject to wild fluctuations in stock prices.

4: BUDGETARY IMPLICATIONS

1. These two aspects are, of course, interrelated because the government's net wealth position is identical to the discounted value of the government's net income stream.
2. Alternatively, the funds could reduce outstanding borrowing, with equivalent effect.
3. It is however possible that the asset shift could have an impact on the economy, with some corresponding fiscal effects.
4. This is based on the assumption the privatisation is not accompanied by a change in the tax regime that, for example would result in the privatised company paying higher corporate profit tax rates. In this case, the government might be willing to accept a reduction in the sales price up to the discounted value of the expected stream of additional profit tax remittances.
5. Bös, (1988), p. 14.
6. See Wattleworth, (1988) for the role of subsidies in government lending programmes.
7. The IMF's *A Manual on Government Finance Statistics*

suggests that sales proceeds should be reflected above the line in a reduction in 'government net lending' (e.g., lending minus repayments) since the budget category of repayments includes any receipts arising from equities sold (IMF, 1986). In terms of the government's balance sheet, assuming no change in other revenue or expenditure, the government's holding of financial assets increases (or its debt decreases) and its holding of equity in the enterprise falls.

8. It may be more appropriate for the evaluation of macroeconomic policies to consider the sale of an enterprise as akin to the sale of government bonds, and regard the sale proceeds as inflows financing the government deficit rather than reducing it. Alternatively, the overall budget deficit could be supplemented by other indicators, such as the net wealth of the government. See Heller, Haas, and Mansur (1986).

9. The only exception would conceivably be if the proceeds financed higher productive expenditures or tax cuts that offered reasonable certainty of a future fiscal benefit.

10. For a more extensive analysis of government activities in a portfolio framework, see Schiller, (1983).

11. For a review of recent developments in debt-equity swaps, see Blackwell and Nocera, 1988.

12. In New Zealand, the fiscal deficit was as high as 9 per cent of GDP in 1983-4 although it has fallen in recent years, achieving a cash balance surplus of 1 per cent in 1987-8. In Ireland, the deficit was above 11 per cent of GDP through 1986, though it has dropped sharply in the last two years. Government interest outlays are approximately 18-20 per cent of expenditure in both countries, and 8-11 per cent of GDP. The ratio of public debt to GDP in Ireland is substantially higher than New Zealand, at 124 per cent in 1987 relative to about 70 per cent.

13. These include the Airways Corporation of New Zealand Ltd, Coal Corporation of New Zealand Ltd., Electricity Corporation of New Zealand, Ltd, Government Life Insurance Corporation Ltd, Government Property Services Ltd, Land Corporations Ltd, New Zealand Forestry Corporation Ltd, New Zealand Post Ltd, Post Office Bank

Ltd and Telecom Corporation of New Zealand Ltd. Two other enterprises, the Work and Development Services Corporation and the Government Computing Service Ltd were established in 1988.

14. In principle, such noncommercial objectives are separately accounted for, but in practice this may not be the case.

15. A clear statement of government policy in this regard can be found in Chapter 11 of the Government's White Paper on Industrial Policy, 1984.

REFERENCES

PRIVATISATION — AN OVERVIEW
BAILEY, E., 'Price and Productivity Change Following Deregulation: the U.S. Experience', *Economic Journal,* 1986.

CABLE, J.R., 'Organisational Form and Economic Performance', in S. Thompson, and M. Wright, *Internal Organisation, Efficiency and Profit,* Oxford: Philip Allen, 1988.

LEIBENSTEIN, H., 'X-Inefficiency and Allocative Inefficiency', *American Economic Review,* 1966.

MILLWARD, R.A. and PARKER, D.M., 'Public and Private Enterprise: Comparative Behaviour and Relative Efficiency', in R.A. Millward, *et al., Public Sector Economics,* London: Longman, 1983.

NISKANEN, W., *Bureaucracy and Representative Government,* Chicago: Aldane, 1971.

VICKERS, J., and YARROW G., *Privatisation: an Economic Analysis,* Cambridge (Mass.) and London: 1988.

WILLIAMSON, O.E., *Corporate Form and Business Behaviour: an Inquiry into the Effects of Organisational Form on Enterprise Behaviour,* New York: Prentice Hall, 1970.

PROMISES AND PITFALLS
AHARONI, Y., *The Evolution and Management of State-owned Enterprises,* Cambridge, (Mass.): Ballinger Publishing Co., 1986.

ALCHIAN, A., 'The Basis of Some Recent Advances in the

Theory of Management of the Firm', *Journal of Industrial Economics,* November, 1965.

AYLEN, J., 'Privatisation in Developing Countries', *Lloyds Bank Review* 163 (January 1987) pp. 15-30.

BACKHAUS, J., 1976. 'Ökonomik der Sozialisierung: Massstäbe und ihre Anwendung an Hand eines internationalen Vergleichs' und 'Bemerkungen zu einer Bibliographie der Sozialisierungstheorie', *Sozialisierung von Unternehmen, Bedingungen und Begruendungen: Vier rechts- und wirt-schaftswissenschaftlichen Studien,* Gerd Winter, Europäische Verlagsanstalt, Frankfurt; 1976 pp. 25-119.

BACKHAUS, J., *Öffentliche Unternehmen: Zum Wirtschaftsrecht, den Funktionen und Rechtsformen offentlicher Unternehmen,* Frankfurt/Main: Haag und Herchen Verlag, 1977/80.

BACKHAUS, J. and WAGNER R., 'The Cameralists: A Public Choice Perspective', *Public Choice* 53 (1987) pp.3-20.

BAILEY, R., 'Privatising Electricity in the United Kingdom — Problems in Store', *Privatisation and Nationalisation,* pp.38-52.

BEESLEY, M. and LITTLECHILD, S., 'Privatisation: Principle, Problems and Priorities', *Lloyds Bank Review* (July 1983), pp.1-20.

BLANKART, C.B., 'Limites de la privatisation des services publics', *Recherches Economiques de Louvain,* vol. 52, no. 2, 1986 pp.117-28.

BLANKART, C.B., 'Eléments d'une theorie economique de la privatisation', *Révue suisse d'Economie politique et de Statistique,* 122 annee, no. 3, 1987.

BLANKART, C.B., 'Limits to Privatisation', *European Economic Review* 31 (1987) pp. 346-351.

BLANKART, C.B., 'Privatisierung im Postwesen: Möglichkeiten und Grenzen', *Privatisierung natürlicher Monopole im Bereich von Bahn, Post und Telecommunikation,* Rupert Windisch, ed., Tuebingen: Mohr/Siebeck, 1987.

BOORSMA, P.B., 'Privatisering', *Openbare Uitgaven 16*, 1984, pp.282-303.

BÖS, D. and PETERS, W., 'A Normative Approach to Privatisation', *Sonderforschungsbereich 303*, Bonn: Rheinische Friedrich-Wilhelms-Universität Bonn, 1987.

BÖS, D., 'A Theory of Privatisation of Public Enterprises', *Journal of Economics* (1986) pp. 17-40.

BÖS, D., 'Privatisation of Public Enterprises', *European Economic Review* 31 (1987) pp.352-60.

BÖS, D., 'Privatisation of Public Firms: A Government-Trade Union Private Shareholder Cooperative Game', *Sonderforschungsbereich 303* Bonn: Rheinische Friedrich-Wilhelms-Universität Bonn, 1987.

BÖS, D., 'Welfare Effects of Privatising Public Enterprises', *Sonderforschungsbereich 303*, Bonn: Rheinische Friedrich-Wilhelms-Universität Bonn, 1986.

BÖS, D., *Public Enterprise Economics: Theory and Application,* Amsterdam: North-Holland, 1986.

BÖS, J.M. and MOLENKAMP, R., 'Privatisering van buitensport-accomodaties', Min. van WVC, Rijswijk, 1985 pp.11-21.

CHEUNG. S., *The Theory of Share Teneancy,* Chicago: University of Chicago Press, 1969.

COKK, P., and PATRICK, C.C., eds., *Privatisation in Less Developed Countries,*

COX, H., 'Thesen zur künftigen Struktur der Deutschen Bundespost', *Beiträge zur öffentlichen Wirtschaft und Gemeinwirtschaft* 2, Berlin: Gesellschaft für öffentliche Wirtschaft und Gemeinwirtschaft, 1988.

EDELMAN, M., *Political Language: Words That Succeed and Policies That Fail,* New York: Academic Press, 1977.

EHEBERG, K.T.R. von, *Finanzen und Finanzwirtschaft.* 'Hand-wörterbuch der Staatswissenschaften', III, Jena: Gustav Fischer, 1900 pp. 902-36.

EHEBERG, K.T.R. von, *Finanzwissenschaft,* Leipzig: Deichert Schup Verlagsbuchhandlung, 1922.

ENGELS, W. *et al.,* 'More Competition in Telecommunications', Bad Homburg: Frankfurter Institut für wirtschaftspolitische Forschung e.V., 1988.

FRANKE, G., 'Economic Analysis of Debt-Equity-Swaps', *Sonderforschungsbereich 178,* Konstanz; Universität Konstanz, 1987.

FRIEDMANN, W., 'Governmental (Public) Enterprises, the International Encyclopaedia of Comparative Law' 1972, Vol. XIII, ch. 13.

GALLONI, N., 'La materia delle privatizzazioni tra economia, politica e ideologia', Rome: manuscript, 1988.

GOLDSCHEID, R., *Staatssozialismus oder Staatskapitalismus. Ein Finanzsoziologischer Beitrag zur Lösung des Staatsschuldenproblems,* Vienna-Leipzig: Anzengruber, 1917.

GRAHAM, C., and PROSSER, T., 'Privatising Nationalised Industries: Constitutional Issues and new legal Techniques', *The Modern Law Review,* (January 1987) pp. 16-51.

HANKE, S.H., *Privatisation: Theory, Evidence and Implementation,* Auburn: Ludwig von Mises Institute, 1986.

HANKE, S.H., ed., *Privatisation and Development,* San Francisco: Institute for Contemporary Studies, 1987.

HEMSTEAD H., Harvester Whitcheaf, 1988.

HER MAJESTY'S TREASURY, *Privatisation in the United Kingdom, background briefing,* London, 1987.

HIRSCH, W.Z., and HARDING, R., 'Contracting-out: A Literature Review', Vancouver: paper, 1987.

Jahrbucher für Nationalökonomie und Statislik, 1899.

LEXIS, W., essay in Conrad, *Handwörterbuch der Staatswissenschaft,* 1901.

LIPSEY, R.G., and LANCASTER, K., 'The General Theory of the Second Best', *Review of Economic Studies* (1956-7) pp. 11-32.

LITTLECHILD, S.C., 'Ten Steps to Denationalisation', *Economic Affairs* (October 1981), pp. 11-19.

McCORMICK, R.E, and TOLLISON, R.D., *Politicians, Legislation, and the Economy: An Inquiry into the Interest Group Theory of Government*, Boston, The Hague, London: Martinus Nijhoff Publishing, 1981.

MOLITOR, B., 'Vermögenspolitik', *Handwörterbuch der Wirtschafts-wissenschaft 8*, Tübingen: Mohr/Siebeck, 1980 pp.282-92.

MORLOK, E.K., 'The Privatisation of urban Transit', *Proceedings of the Transportation Forum*, 1987.

MUSOLF, L., *Uncle Sam's Private, Profitseeking Corporations*, Toronto: D.C. Heath and Co., 1983.

NEWMAN, K., *The Selling of British Telecom*, New York: St. Martins, 1986.

NEWOTNY, E., *Der öffentliche Sektor: Einführung in die Finanzwissenschaft*, Berlin, Heidelberg, New York: Springer, 1987.

PRISCHING, M., 'Zur politischen Symbolik einer Reprivatisierungspolitik einige Randbemerkungen', Maastricht: manuscript, 1988.

PROSSER, T., 'Privatised Industries and Government in the United Kingdom', *Capitalism, Culture and Regulation*, manuscript, 1987.

PROSSER, T., 'Regulation of privatised Enterprises: Institutions and Procedures', ibid.

PUVIANI, A., Teoria dell'Illusione Finanziaria, Milano-Palermo-Napoli 1903: deutsch u.d.T.: *Die Illusionen in der öffentlichen Finanzwirtschaft, Finanzwissenschaftliche Forschungsarbeiten*, N.F., H. 22, Berlin, 1960.

RIMPLER, 'Geschichte der Domänen' in *Handwörterbuch der Staatswissenschaften*, III, Jena: Gustav Fischer, pp.194-205.

RUTTEN, F.F.H., 'Privatisering en deregulering in de gezondheidszorg', *Openbare Uitgaven 15*, 1983 pp.328-43.

SAMUELSON, P.A., 'The Pure Theory of Public Expenditure', *Review of Economics and Statistics* 36 (1954) pp.387-89.

SMITH, A., *A Wealth of Nations,* London: Everyman's Library, 1970.

SPINDLER, Z.A., "Bricking-up" Government Bureaus and Crown Corporations: The Economics of Privatisation' T.M. Ohashi and T.P. Roth, *Privatisation: Theory & Practice,* Vancouver: The Fraser Institute, 1980 pp. 153-79.

SPINDLER, Z.A., and WALKER, M.A., 'The Tax Reform Cycle Canadian Tax Reform as Public Goods', paper, 1988.

SPINDLER, Z.A., 'A Rent-seeking Perspective on Privatization', paper, 1989.

STEEL, D. and HEALD, D., eds, *Privatising Public Enterprises: Options and Dilemmas,* Royal Institute of Public Administration, 1984.

STIGLITZ, J.E., *Economics of the Public Sector* (2nd ed.), New York: Norton, 1988.

THIEMEYER, T., and QUADEN, G., eds. 'The Privatisation of Public Enterprises: A European Debate', *Annals of Public and Co-operative Economy,* Liege: Ciriec, 1986.

VELJANOVSKI, C. and BENTLEY, M., *Selling the State: Privatisation in Britain,* London: Weidenfeld and Nicolson, 1987.

VELTHOVEN, B.C.J. van, and WINDEN, F.A.A.M. van, 'Privatisering, een politiek-economische benadering', *Openbare Uitgaven 16* (1984) pp.304-17.

VICKERS, J., and YARROW, G., *Privatisation: Economic Analysis,* Cambridge (Mass.) MIT Press, 1988.

WINDISCH, R., ed., *Privatisierung natuerlicher Monopole im Bereich von Bahn, Post und Telekommunikation,* Tübingen: J.C.B. Mohr (Paul Siebeck), 1987.

BUDGETARY IMPACT

ATKINSON, P., *Reform of Public Sector Trading Activities: Reflections on the New Zealand Experience,* Unpublished IFC paper, 1988.

BARRINGTON, T.J., 'Public Enterprise in Ireland', *Annals of Public and Cooperative Economy* 56 (July/September, 1985), pp. 287-311.

BLACKWELL, M. AND NOCERA, S., 'Developing Countries Develop Debt-Equity Swap Programs to Manage External Debt,' *IMF Survey* (June 1988), pp.226-28.

BÖS, D., *Arguments on Privatisation,* Cologne: unpublished June 1988.

BUCKLAND, R., 'The Costs and Returns of the Privatisation of Nationalized Industries', *Public Administration,* 65 (Autumn, 1987), pp. 241-57.

CANDOY-SEKSE, R., *Techniques of Privatisation of State-Owned Enterprises,*Vol. III, World Bank Technical Paper No. 90., Washington, World Bank, 1988.

DALMOAK, M., 'Stock Market: Boost from Privatisation', *The Banker* No. 135 (April 1985).

HELLER, P.S., HAAS, R.D. and MANSUR, A.H., *A Review of the Fiscal Impulse Measure,* Occasional Paper No. 44, Washington: International Monetary Fund, May 1986.

HEMMING, R. and MANSOOR, A., *Privatisation and Public Enterprises,* Occasional Paper No. 56, Washington: International Monetary Fund, January 1988.

INTERNATIONAL MONETARY FUND, *A Manual on Government Finance Statistics,* Washington 1986.

IRELAND, GOVERNMENT OF, *White Paper on Industrial Policy,* Dublin: Stationary Office, 1984.

KAY, J.A., and THOMPSON, D.J., 'Privatisation: A Policy in Search of a Rationale', *Economic Journal,* 96 (March 1986), pp.18-32.

MANSOOR, A., 'The Budgetary Impact of Privatisation' in Mario I. Blejer and Ke-young Chu, eds, *Measurement of Fiscal Impact — Methodological Issues* Occasional Paper 59, Washington: International Monetary Fund, June 1988, pp. 48-56.

MAYER, C. and MEADOWCROFT, S., 'Selling Public Assets: Techniques and Financial Implications', *Fiscal Studies* 6(4), pp. 42-56.

MOLONEY, M.G., 'Privatisation', *The Irish Banking Review,* (September 1983), pp. 44-52.

NELLIS, J. and KIKERI, S., 'The Privatisation of Public Enterprises', *World Development,* 1989.

NEW ZEALAND, THE TREASURY, (a) *Government Management: Brief to the Incoming Government, 1987,* vol. 1, Wellington: August 1987, pp. 96-117.

NEW ZEALAND, THE TREASURY, (b) *Budget 1988,* (Part 1 Speech), Wellington, 1988.

NEW ZEALAND, DEPARTMENT OF STATISTICS, (c) *Official Yearbook, 1988-89,* Wellington: October 1988.

OECD, *Economic Survey, New Zealand,* Paris; April 1989.

'PRICING THE PRIVATISED', *The Economist* (30 July, 1988), p. 65.

SCHILLER, C., *Staatsausgaben und Crowding-Out Effekte,* Frankfurt am Main: Peter Lang, 1983.

SWEENEY, P., 'Public Enterprise Profitability Increases while Employment Decreases', *The Irish Times* (1 February, 1989), p. 16.

VICKERS, J. and YARROW, G., *Privatisation: An Economic Analysis,* Cambridge (Mass.): MIT Press, 1988.

VULYSTEKE, C., *Techniques of Privatisation of State-Owned Enterprises,* Vol. 1, World Bank Technical Paper No. 88, Washington: World Bank, 1988.

WATTLEWORTH, M., 'Credit Subsidies in Budgetary Lending: Computation, Effects and Fiscal Implications' in Mario I. Blejer and Ke-young Chu, op. cit., pp.57-68.

YARROW, G., 'Privatisation in Theory and Practice', *Economic Policy* 1 (1986), pp. 324-77.

PRIVATISATION AND SOCIAL INSURANCE

ATKINSON, A.B., 'Social Insurance and Income Maintenance', Discussion Paper no. 11, ST/CERD Welfare State Programme, London School of Economics, 1986.

BLACKWELL, John, *Unemployment Compensation and Work Incentives,* Background Paper No. 2, Report of the Commission on Social Welfare, 1986.

BLACKWELL, John, 'Family Income Support: Policy Options' in Sean Healy and Brigid Reynolds, *Family Income Support,* Dublin: CMRS, 1988.

CENTRAL STATISTICS OFFICE, *National Income and Expenditure 1988,* Dublin: Stationery Office, 1989.

COMMISSION ON SOCIAL WELFARE, *Report,* Dublin: Stationery Office, 1986.

DANZIGER, S., HAVEMAN, R. AND PLOTNICK, R., 'How income transfers affect work, savings and the income distribution: a critical review', *Journal of Economic Literature,* Vol. , 19, No. 3 (1981) 975-1028.

DANZIGER, Sheldon and SMOLENSKY, Eugene, 'Income Transfers and the Poor: A Cross-National Perspective', *Journal of Social Policy,* Vol. 14, No. 3, (1985) 257-262.

DEPARTMENT OF SOCIAL WELFARE, *A National Income-related Pension Scheme — A Discussion Paper,* Dublin: Stationery Office, 1976.

DESMOND, B., Address at First Annual Conference of the Retirement Planning Council of Ireland, 17 October, 1985.

DISNEY, Richard, 'Statutory Sick Pay: An Appraisal', *Fiscal Studies,* Vol. 8, No. 2 (1987).

HUGHES, Gerard, *Social Insurance and Absence from Work in Ireland,* Dublin: The Economic and Social Research Institute, 1982.

HUGHES, Gerard, *Disability Benefit Reform: Rationalisation or Subsidisation?* Dublin: The Economic and Social Research Institute, 1988.

LE GRAND, Julian and ROBINSON, Ray, 'Privatisation and the

Welfare State: An Introduction', in Julian Le Grand & Ray Robinson, eds., *Privatisation and the Welfare State,* London: Allen and Unwin, 1984.

OECD, *The Future of Social Protection,* Paris: OECD, 1988.

O'HIGGINS, Michael, 'Welfare, Redistribution, and Inequality — Disillusion, Illusion and Reality' in Philip Bean, John Ferris and David Whynes, eds, *In Defence of Welfare,* London: Tavistock, 1985.

ROTTMAN, David B., and REIDY, Mairéad, 'Redistribution through State Social Expenditure in the Republic of Ireland: 1973-1980', Report No. 85, National Economic and Social Council, 1988.

SAUNDERS, Peter, 'Evidence on Income Redistribution by Governments', Working Paper No. 11, Economics and Statistics Department, OECD, 1984.

SAWYER, Malcolm, 'Income Distribution and the Welfare State', in Andrea Boltho, ed., *The European Economy: Growth and Crisis*, Oxford University Press, 1982.

TRANSPORT DEREGULATION AND PRIVATISATION
BAILEY, Elizabeth E., and WILLIAMS, Jeffrey R., 'Sources of Rent in The Deregulated Airline Industry', *Journal of Law and Economics*, Vol. XXXI (April 1988).

BARRETT, Sean D., *Transport Policy in Ireland*, Irish Management Institute, 1982.

BARRETT, Sean D., *Airports for Sale — The Case of Competition*, Adam Smith Institute, 1984.

BARRETT, Sean D., *Flying High, Airline Prices and European Regulation*, Avebury, 1987.

BARRETT, Sean D., 'European Air Transport: Uncabin the Consumer', *Journal of Economic Affairs*, (January 1988).

BARRETT, Sean D., 'Europe's Contested Airspace — Time for Market Solutions', *Journal of Economic Affairs*, (June/July 1989).

BAUMOL, W.J., 'Contestable Markets: An Uprising in the Theory of Industrial Structure', *American Economic Review,* (March 1983).

BAYFIELD, K., 'Competition and Regulation in Privatising the British Airports Authority', *Public Money*, General Series 4, 1984.

BUCHANAN, J., *Public Finance In Democratic Process*, University of North Carolina, 1987.

BURTON, J., *Picking Losers — the Political Economy of Industrial Policy*, London: Institute of Economic Affairs, 1983, ch. 1.

CIE, *Report on Internal Public Transport* (The Pacemaker Report), 1963.

CIVIL AVIATION AUTHORITY, *Airline Competition Policy* (1984) Cap. 500, p.16.

CIVIL AVIATION AUTHORITY, *Report of the Monopolies and Mergers Commission: Second Response of the Civil Aviation Authority*, (1985)Cap. 599, p. 1.

CIVIL AVIATION AUTHORITY, *Competition on the Main Domestic Trunk Routes*, (1987) Paper 87005, Table 26.

CONROY, J.C., *A History of Railways in Ireland*, Longman Green, 1928, p.370.

DEMSETZ, H., 'Why Regulate Utilities?', *Journal of Law and Economics*, (April 1968).

DOWNS, A., *An Economic Theory of Democracy*, Harper and Row, 1957.

DOWNS, A., *Inside Bureaucracy,* Little and Brown, 1967.

Dublin Docks Review Group Report, Chairman John M. Horgan, Dublin: The Labour Court, 1984, ch.6.

FOSTER, C., 'Privatising Britain's Airports: What's to be Gained?', in Bayfield, K., op. cit.

GOTCH, J., 'The Private Dimension', *Transport*, (June 1987).

KAHN, A., 'Surprises of Airline Deregulation', *American Economic Review*, (March 1988).

KELSEY, A., 'How the Stock Market Sees Transport', *Transport*, (February 1986).

KILVINGTON, R.P., *Lessons of the 1980 Transport Act*, mimeograph, Oxford: Transport Studies Unit, 1985.

LAZAURS, P., (1984), 'UK Transport Development — Making the Most of the Private Purse', *Transport*, (March/April 1984).

LEVINE, M., 'Airline Competition in Deregulated Markets: Theory, Firms' Strategy and Public Policy', *Yale Journal on Regulation*, (Spring 1987).

MEENAN, James, *The Irish Economy Since 1920*, Liverpool University Press, 1970.

MONOPOLIES AND MERGERS COMMISSION, *The Civil Aviation Authority*, 1983.

MONOPOLIES AND MERGERS COMMISSION, *The British Airports Authority*, 1985.

MORRISON, H., *Socialisation and Transport*, Constable, 1983.

NATIONAL PRICES COMMISSION, Occasional Paper 10, 1973, p. 45.

NISKANEN, W., *Bureaucracy — Servant or Master*, Institute of Economic Affairs, 1973.

PRICE WATERHOUSE, *Privatisation: The Facts*, 1987.

SCHULTZE, C., 'Industrial Policy — A Dissent', *Brookings Institute Bulletin*, (Fall 1983).

STARKIE, D., 'British Railways: Opportunities for a Contestable Market', in Kay, Mayer and Thompson, *Privatisation and Regulation, The UK Experience*, Clarendon, 1986 ch. 9.

STIGLER, G., 'The Theory of Economic Regulation, *Bell Journal of Economics*, 1971 pp. 335-58.

TRANSPORT POLICY — A GREEN PAPER, Dublin: Government Publications, November 1985.

TRIBUNAL ON PUBLIC TRANSPORT REPORT, Dublin: Government Publications, 1939.

TULLOCK G., *Private Wants, Public Means: An Economic Analysis of the Desirable Scope of Government,* Basic Books, 1970.

TULLOCK, G., *Toward a Theory of the Rent-Seeking Society,* Texas: A & M Press, 1980.

VICKERS, J. and YARROW, G., *Privatisation: an Economic Analysis,* Cambridge (Mass.): MIT Press, 1988.

ENERGY AND PRIVATISATION
BUNN, Derek, and VLAHOS, Kiriakos, 'Evaluation of the Nuclear Constraint in a Privatised Electricity Supply Industry', *Fiscal Studies,* Vol. 10, No. 1 (February, 1989).

COMMISSION OF THE EUROPEAN COMMUNITIES, *Towards Completion of the Internal Market for Natural Gas,* Proposal for a Council Directive on the transit of natural gas through the major systems. COM (89) 334 Final — SYN 206, Brussels: (6 September 1989).

CONVERY, F., *State Assets and Private Enterprise; Issues in the Theory and Practice of Privatisation in Ireland.* Working Paper No. 40. Resource and Environmental Policy Centre, University College, Dublin, March 1987.

ECONOMIST, *Petrol Prices, Why Down Means Up,* 25 March, 1989.

FT International Gas Report (1989), *How to make the figures add up the right way when you don't have any figures at all.* August 31, 138/15.

HAMMOND, B., Helm D. and Thompson D., 'British Gas Options for Privatisation', *Fiscal Studies,* Vol. 6, No. 4, (November, 1985).

HELM, Dieter, 'Regulating the Electricity Supply Industry', *Fiscal Studies,* Vol. 9, No. 3, (August, 1988.)

NATIONAL DEVELOPMENT PLAN 1989-1993, Dublin: Stationery Office, 1989.

PETROLEUM ECONOMIST, *Independent Storage, A Vital Service Industry,* G. Vernon Hough, (January, 1988).

PETROLEUM ECONOMIST, *World Refineries Survey, Better Prospects Downstream*, Martin Quinlan, (September, 1989).

PRYKE, Richard, 'Privatising Electricity Generation', *Fiscal Studies*, Vol. 8, No. 3, (August, 1987).

ROBINSON, Colin, 'Privatising the Energy Industries', in C. Veljanovski, ed., *Privatisation and Competition, a Market Prospective,* Institute of Economic Affairs, Hobart Paperback 28, 1989.

STELZER, I., *'Privatisation and Regulation: Oft-Necessary Complements'* in C. Veljanovski, op.cit.